PRAISE FOR
NEIGHBORS AND WISE MEN

"*Neighbors and Wise Men* is the 'red pill' for people like us who are trying to make a difference. In a stunning missionary reversal, Tony Kriz's testimony offers us a courageous gift that may save our lives. I read it from front-to-back in one sitting. I swallowed the stories, and my eyes were opened to the Spirit's movement in my own life through the most unlikely people and places."

— Paul Sparks
Co-Director of Parish Collective

"Wow. *Neighbors and Wise Men* manages to capture the magic of sitting face to face with my friend Tony Kriz—an exceptionally warm, curious, and engaging conversationalist. Many people have speculated about what practicing the way of Jesus might look like in the changing landscape of the 21st century. Instead of theorizing, Tony invites us into his heart, his life, his wounds, and his relationships to help us imagine what is possible. His storytelling is ruthlessly honest and infinitely hopeful."

— Mark Scandrette
Author of *Soul Graffiti* and
Practicing the Way of Jesus

"In *Neighbors and Wise Men* Tony jumps off the page, as real in black and white as he is in life: intense, funny, wicked smart, and somehow equally kind and tender. Tony would tell you he's just another guy asking soul-searching questions (with an ample dose of self-deprecating humor) but I know better. In the church we are becoming and we need more leaders like Tony, and more stories like these of men and women who are willing to lay their failures alongside their triumphs so that we may learn together. Fortunately, he not only lives these questions well, it turns out he can write, too, and that's good for all of us."

— Penny Gruener Carothers
Social Justice Editor, Burnside
Writers Collective

"These stories and reflections pulse with heart, humility, insight, and inspiration. *Neighbors and Wise Men* is exactly the book we've been waiting for from the fascinating figure we met in *Blue Like Jazz*, and who we sensed had so much more to say and share. The wait is over."

— Tom Krattenmaker
USA Today Board of Contributors
Author of *Onward Christian Athletes* and *The Evangelicals You Don't Know*

"Books have the power to change the way we see the world around us, and more importantly, the way we live our lives. Tony Kriz's *Neighbors and Wise Men* is just such a book. Disillusioned after years on the mission field, Kriz returned to the States to discover that God could speak to Him—and all of us—in the most unlikely of places, and through the most unlikely of people. This extraordinary book will inspire you to keep your eyes peeled for God's presence everywhere you turn."

— Joseph Anfuso
Founder and President of Forward Edge International
Author of *Message in a Body* and *Serendestiny*

"This book is a spritz of Windex™ on the murky lens of life. It invites us to see the presence of God in the glorious mundane. Tony's unconventional journey finds voice in *Neighbors and Wise Men*, blending honest spirituality with extraordinary skill as a storyteller. I already want to re-read this book."

— Dwight J. Friesen
Associate Professor of Practical Theology, The Seattle School of Theology & Psychology
Author of *Thy Kingdom Connected*

"Tony Kriz is an authentic prophetic voice among a new generation of loyal radicals. Tony does not write as a romantic idealist, but as one who has been tested by life, and whose faith has deepened and evolved through love and suffering. His book is a gift to those who are in the midst of, or have ever experienced, a crisis of faith. But beware, this is also a dangerous book, one that crosses our usual boundaries of who is 'in' and who is 'out.' Tony turns evangelism inside out, like Jesus did."

— Carole Dale Spencer
Associate Professor of Christian
Spirituality, Earlham School of
Religion

"Jesus knew that his Father was constantly communicating. This is why Jesus cared about people having *ears to hear*. He knew everyone had flaps of flesh on the side of their heads. That was not the point. The point is this: most of us do not have ears *to hear*. We have ears to filter and manage information in order to fit it within our current viewpoints. Or we have ears to win arguments. Tony Kriz teaches us to listen to God by *hearing* the surprisingly wise people in our everyday, ordinary lives. Learning to be alert to God in this way is central to our spiritual growth and the key to spiritual conversations of all kinds."

— Todd Hunter
Bishop, The Anglican Church in
North America
Author of *Our Favorite Sins*

"*Neighbors and Wise Men* is an outstanding read. From missionary work in Albania to being embedded at highly secular Reed College to hanging out in the neighborhood English pub, again and again Tony has chosen to search for meaning—and for Christ—in some of the most complicated and unlikely intersections available. Because of his ability to honestly observe and articulately reflect on his own experiences and struggles, the reader gets the benefit of the fascinating journey Tony has been on. A wonderful book—the one I'd always hoped Tony Kriz would write."

— Dan Merchant
Author of *Lord, Save Us From Your Followers*

"I love stories, especially ones perceptively told—revealing human yearning, divine pursuit, and personal change. Those are the kinds I can't put down. My friend Tony Kriz tells his brilliantly. *Neighbors and Wise Men* is rich with keen, nuanced insight, character growth, and gospel transformation spread throughout like compost tilled into the garden. Whether being scolded by a Muslim grandmother in Albania or confessing doubt to a bartender in a Portland pub, or being preached at by Garrett about 'living local,' Tony sees God's grace enriching the dirt surrounding every relationship and interaction. His story opened my eyes to see the nourishing soil and beauty of the garden of unexpected wise men and neighbors in my life. As a result, I am seeing more clearly God's comprehensive pursuit of me, my family, and all people. Thank you Tony!"

— Clark Blakeman
Executive Director at Second
Stories

"Tony Kriz gives the reader a peak into his divine encounters with the other and how these encounters shaped his life. Kriz's stories comfort us in our shared broken humanity and challenge us to new understandings of what it means to live an authentically spiritual life. His self-deprecating humor twinned with his narrative panache will keep the reader suspended between a smile and a tear. With his first offering, *Neighbors and Wise Men*, Kriz exhibits an ease with the pen that poises him to become a prominent storyteller of our time. One ponders what might come next!"

— Dr. Deborah Koehn Loyd

"Socrates said, 'The unexamined life is not worth living.' I say, 'The examined life is worth sharing.' Especially if it's as interesting and well told as Tony's."

— Mike Hamel
Author of *Stumbling Toward Heaven*

"I enjoyed walking with Tony through his self-induced failures and reluctant epiphanies. He tells his stories with a charm and grace that foreshadow the outcome. *Neighbors and Wise Men* challenges me to see God present in and through every relationship today. They remind me to pay attention, die to self, and trust in God's purpose and direction. They invite an intentionality of faith that is rich, relational, and redemptive; as if we live in a world saturated with the presence of a transcendent Deity who cares deeply to be known by us, and for us to know Him, and each other."

— Phil Long
Founder of the Sacrificial Poet
Project
Creator of the Jesus Poetry Slam

"God speaks to us from the mouths of strangers, unclean messengers, outcasts, even the inanimate, so we can't sanction what's being said. We can't easily reproduce it or schedule it for a repeat performance. On his way to unexpected places Tony joins some wonderful traveling companions."

— Lee Cantelon
Hollywood and New York Film and
Music Producer
Author of *The Words*

"I love Tony. He is my friend. His story is a beautiful odyssey—messy, exotic, passionate, intelligent, filled with passion. For me, as a Lakota follower of Jesus, theologizing is 'storytelling'. Tony's story is a theological tale of possibilities of hope, love, truth, and light in Jesus for a broken humanity. It is a human story. I believe those who read this will find themselves in his story too; discovering hope and the courage to not settle. He doesn't create the illusion that Jesus is found in convenient propositions which bring about a sanitized end to all of our problems. He invites us to be fully human."

— Richard Twiss, Sicangu Lakota
President, Wiconi International

"*Neighbors and Wise Men* by Tony Kriz is the antithesis to much of today's Christian writing, which is chock full of cool slogans and catchy acronyms. Rawness, authenticity, and honest reflection ooze out of every page of *Neighbors and Wise Men*. This book is not about success. It's about a faithfulness that compels Kriz to continue moving into the unknown, no matter the cost. I consider it an honor to have read this book and am very appreciative Kriz had the boldness to pen these words for all to experience."

— Andrew Marin
Author of *Love Is an Orientation*
(www.themarinfoundation.org)

"*Neighbors and Wise Men* chronicles an authentic life journey that reveals God's image and reflection in many people and places. Tony Kriz tells his story as well as the stories of those he encounters along the way in an engaging and captivating manner. You will be encouraged and challenged by the honest questions and paradoxes revealed in the words and lives of neighbors and wise men."

— Andrea P. Cook, Ph.D.
President, Warner Pacific College

"Each one of us is fearfully and wonderfully made by our creator. He knows us very personally and intimately and He oftentimes speaks to us through our conscience and conscientiousness in a language that is uniquely of Him. But too often, because of the message bearer, we have been trained to not listen. *Neighbors and Wise Men* is a clear example of awakening to the language that God speaks, never mind the messenger. I highly recommend reading this book; it will awaken you to understanding His language to you."

— Clifford O. Chappell
Pastor, St. Johns All Nations
Church of God in Christ

NEIGHBORS

and

WISE MEN

NEIGHBORS

and

WISE MEN

SACRED ENCOUNTERS
IN A PORTLAND PUB
and OTHER
UNEXPECTED PLACES

TONY KRIZ

THOMAS NELSON
Since 1798

NASHVILLE   DALLAS   MEXICO CITY   RIO DE JANEIRO

Published in Nashville, Tennessee, by Thomas Nelson. Thomas Nelson is a registered trademark of Thomas Nelson, Inc.

Author is represented by the literary agency of Credo Communications, Grand Rapids, Michigan, www.credocommunications.net.

Thomas Nelson, Inc., titles may be purchased in bulk for educational, business, fundraising, or sales promotional use. For information, please e-mail SpecialMarkets@ ThomasNelson.com.

Unless otherwise indicated, Scripture quotations are taken from the Holy Bible, New International Version®, NIV®. Copyright © 1973, 1978, 1984, 2011 by Biblica, Inc.™ Used by permission of Zondervan. All rights reserved worldwide. www.zondervan.com

Scripture quotations marked NASB are taken from the NEW AMERICAN STANDARD BIBLE®. © The Lockman Foundation 1960, 1962, 1963, 1968, 1971, 1972, 1973, 1975, 1977, 1995. Used by permission.

Scripture quotations marked MSG are taken from *The Message* by Eugene H. Peterson. © 1993, 1994, 1995, 1996, 2000. Used by permission of NavPress Publishing Group. All rights reserved.

Library of Congress Cataloging-in-Publication Data

Kriz, Tony.
  Neighbors and wise men : sacred encounters in a Portland pub and other unexpected places / Tony Kriz.
    p. cm.
  Includes bibliographical references.
  ISBN 978-0-8499-4739-1 (trade paper)
  1. Kriz, Tony. 2. Missionaries--Biography. I. Title.
  BV3705.K75A3 2012
  277.3'083092—dc23
  [B]   2012020343

Printed in the United States of America

12 13 14 15 16 17 QG 6 5 4 3 2 1

TO KEVIN,

You are the best example of the truth that friendship transcends tribe, church, faith, or creed. You know me as well as anyone, my good and my bad, and yet you have consistently supported and loved me for more than twenty years now . . . and for a lifetime to come.

CONTENTS

Section Two: Alone and Away

Sootion Throo: Loarning to Rccd

Section Four: Coming Home

FOREWORD

NEW VOICES ARE RISING UP. WHEN WALLS COLLAPSE, SPACE opens and wind is freer in her movements. Books like *Neighbors and Wise Men* are evidence in one genre of these voices. For those of us who have already lived as global nomads and third-culture kids, and for the younger tribal generations rising up who have little comprehension of religious affiliation or political membership, for whom something that actually works matters more than tradition, these changes are an invitation to come surf the storm.

I believe there is a relational God who pilots the ship with a sure and steady love and who invites the participation of the human creation with all its fear and posturing. I experience daily and have growing respect for true and authentic humanity; our ability to learn, love, discover, risk, listen, gather, create, laugh, innovate, pray, communicate, forgive, sing, reconcile, explore, work, play, give, serve, heal, and worship.

> *There is a gathering of the friends*
> *Who sit in smile and stories tell*
> *Of how we live and how we die*
> *And how we rose and how we fell*

The laughter near while tears yet nearer
As inner worlds we turn to light
An offering to each the other
A love that strong resists the flight

Oh hear oh tender heart and soul
You're not alone, you're not alone
For in your words your story too
Is woven with a multitude
With hand in hand who fight the night
'Til all of us are safely home.

(Every human being *is* a story.) This book is simple, because it is story. This book is profound and challenging, because it is story. There is no hidden agenda, which may disappoint some, while there is a painting of real questions, which may offend others. Any offense or disappointment is welcome because it speaks more about the reader invited than the writer creating. So, too, is welcome intro-spection and conversation, self-examination and repentance. May we all humble ourselves to hear what the Spirit is whispering to us, and may we also trust the Spirit in the lives of others.

— Paul Young,
Best-selling author of
The Shack

AUTHOR'S NOTE

IN THE FOLLOWING PAGES YOU ARE GOING TO FIND MY STORIES. They are written with my heart as well as my memory. I am sure that my memories are flawed, made hazy by time. I know some memories are incomplete, so gaps are filled by research and carefully discerned imagination. I have labored to tell these stories accurately. I have tried to represent my friends well. Out of respect, some names have been changed. In hopes of readability, some details have been omitted and a few conversations have been consolidated.

(The people in these stories have changed my life.)They have transformed me and introduced me to a world to which I was mostly blind. I am in their debt. These pages are a testimony to their grace and affection toward me.

It is worth noting that there are thousands of people who are not in the book. Among my glaring omissions are many friends, mentors, and coworkers who profess to be Christians. This narrative tells a specific story, the story of discovering a deeper and broader faith in Jesus from people and in places that are most often considered outside of Christendom.

The Albania section was particularly difficult to write. First, these stories happened almost twenty years ago now. Also, there are innumerable friends from that time who did not fit into the rhythm or scope of this book. I want to acknowledge that I am also forever indebted to my Christian friends and fellow missionaries from those transformative years.

Reed College is the setting of section three, Learning to Reed. With each page I was painfully aware of the popularized stereotypes about this beautiful and amazing college. In the stories, I even wrestle with those stereotypes. To my friends in and from the Reed community, as you read these stories, I pray that you feel my affection and admiration for you and for your school. I hope that some of those stereotypes are righted through these pages.

On the topic of stereotypes, I have no doubt that some will be tempted to assign religious labels to me. If you have any doubts, I want you to know that anyone who walks with me places me very comfortably within the Christian tribe. I love the Trinity. I love my Bible. And most important, I believe that Jesus Christ is absolutely central and essential to the story of the human soul and the great restoration to come.

Let the epiphanies come.

—Be at peace,
Tony

Introduction

====

BORN AGAIN

I CAN'T BELIEVE ANYMORE.

I was living in the last of a series of missionary outposts that had filled most of my twenties. This one left me in the former Yugoslavia, beneath the flight path of NATO war machines preparing to bomb Serbian troops in Kosovo.

This thought, *I can't believe anymore,* had been buried deep inside me for close to a year.

This final outpost was the last stop on what I had often described as a great adventure. It was exotic. I was a driven young man, driven by a desire to make a difference in the world. I was also driven by an obsession to prove myself. I had to prove myself to my church, to my dad, and ultimately to my God.

Obsessions snowball with time. So I took harder and harder assignments in Europe's complicated and pain-filled corners. This drive was both intoxicating and addictive. And like all addictions, it left me with a dead soul.

My last year on the field, I kept this sorrow-secret hidden deep inside me: I had stopped believing.

No one knew. No one could be allowed to know. I would lose my job. I would lose my whole world as I knew it.

What possible place exists for a missionary who doesn't believe?

A cadaver soul impacts everything. It makes faith impossible. It makes prayer impossible. But that is only the beginning.

It also makes kindness almost impossible. It makes true compassion impossible.

In my case, it also led to acts of manipulation, anger, and emotional abuse. It is a great irony that I had been commissioned to support and protect, but instead I became an instrument of hurt and chaos.

In what can best be described as a mercy killing, those under my charge turned me in. They demanded that I be removed from my post and ultimately from the mission field.

———

Months later my leadership finally determined that I needed to return "home" to heal, which meant Oregon, a place I had left long before.

They said I needed to find the faith I had lost.

I was sentenced to a Christian seminary.

I spent the next year, from nine in the morning until two in the afternoon, sitting at plastic-topped tables, under fluorescent lights, surrounded by taupe-colored walls.

I needed my professors to meet me in the very midst of my lost faith.

They couldn't, so I sat silent, like a man in solitary. At the time, I didn't know if I could survive in America, a world I had long forgotten. Academia, strip malls, and big-box stores were like sound pollution after my years in the developing world.

How could I find a way station of relief?

Relief soon came. After class I would escape to a British pub a couple of neighborhoods away from campus. My inner screaming eased in the mostly empty, cavernous, dimly lit, dark-wooded world of the Horse Brass Pub.

Back on campus, I had nothing to offer my fellow students. I did not have the language to explain that I could not share their hope and idealism. It was different at the Horse Brass. My company instead became the sort of nonreligious ragamuffins who frequent a British pub at three in the afternoon.

I had a favorite table. It was under the large, dark-framed window at the pub's north end, my back situated against the street and my face toward the wraparound antique bar. There were thick rafters and rough-hewn pillars on every side. Occasionally, Dennis the bartender would give me a chin nod, and on the really great days, he would come around the bar and sit awhile, often bringing me a joke.

My routine solidified quickly. Dennis would catch my silhouette as I came through the heavy double doors. Most days I couldn't even get to the end of the bar before Dennis had already poured me a chewy India Pale Ale in an English pint. I would collapse behind my computer and thick theology texts, all spread across the long, skinny table. A couple of deep breaths, and then I'd dive into my studies.

Each day, inevitably, someone would come and distract me from my studies. Occasionally the person was tipsy and lonely; usually he was just friendly and bored.

My studies would sit on the table like a quivering puppy, begging to be included in the conversation. They could not be ignored forever. Eventually my pub friends would ask what I was reading or writing. They wanted to know about me. They wanted to hear what I was learning.

I would begin sharing safely, staying in the world of ideas. Eventually, I would tell them about my years overseas.

I talked about my secret sorrow.

I told them that I was a theology student but that I wasn't sure what I believed anymore. This confession always seemed to release delight in my companions. It is funny; after years of having all the answers, (I discovered how attracted people are to someone with honest doubts and real questions.)

This was when something magical would happen. Every time it startled me. They started to counsel me, counsel from their stories, from their hurt, and from their own faithlessness.

I cried out to them. I told them I was at a precipice, at a watershed, teetering on a rooftop: Jesus on one side and the desperate unknown on the other.

The more I would share, the more they would enter my hurt. They would tell me to "fall toward Jesus."

———

Over that next year I did discover faith again. Not only did I find faith; I found a mostly satisfying sort of Jesus-faith, based in a communal God who loves me and suffers for me. This God was creative and unshackled.

This was a God who is, as the Scriptures say, "not far from any one of us; for in him we live and move and have our being." He is "over all and through all and in all" and "in him all things hold together."

This faith I discovered was unapologetically Christian, rooted and dependent upon the holy Scriptures and the historical and global church, but at the same time, fresh and fueled from unexpected sources.

This rebirth did not happen in the classrooms of my religious graduate school. It did not happen in the pew of a local church.

It primarily happened in a nicotine-saturated beer hall.

My priests were not pastors or professors; they were pub folk: people who would never call themselves Christians, nor would they visit a Christian church, but they were the gospel to me all the same.

―――――――

This pub story barely scratches the surface of a much larger journey. Many of my spiritual heroes have been unexpected. Jesus has often taught me to follow him through those who do not bear his name. Much of my growth in the Christian faith has been provoked from places far outside the Christian church.

This is a book of epiphanies: of God encountering a faith-challenged missionary through the people he went to save . . . of Jesus giving a lost seminarian unwitting teachers from unpredictable places . . . of a broken man encountering his Redeemer from voices he had been taught to reject.

This journey continues still. It once challenged me to fly across oceans; today it challenges me to know my neighbor across the street.

Please, sit back. Pour yourself a chewy IPA (or your beverage of choice). I pray you will enjoy these sacred encounters from many unexpected places.

SECTION ONE

LIVING WITH MUSLIMS

THESE FIRST CHAPTERS TAKE PLACE IN THE COUNTRY OF ALBANIA. Albania is a Muslim country. What does that mean? In this case it means that approximately 80 percent of Albanians come from a historically Muslim background. The particular time I arrived in Albania, it was coming out of fifty years of Communism. It was a season of significant social, political, and spiritual discovery. It is out of that soil that this book springs. It is in that world that I met the friends that fill these pages.

1

PILGRIMAGE

I BOUNCED ON TOP OF THE LOOSE SHOCKS OF THE EARLY-MODEL Mercedes-Benz sedan, the ubiquitous choice for taxis all across the developing world. Turkish-sounding music came from the radio. A red flag with a black eagle and gold fringe dangled from the rear-view mirror.

My breathing was shallow . . . part from exhaustion, part from fear, part from a sense of new adventure. We had pulled out of the airport parking lot just minutes before. My first experience of Albania was a thirty-minute taxi ride from the national airport to Tirana, the capital city. My mind was storing its first snapshots of the Albanian countryside outside the backseat window.

It was late afternoon and the sun was low in the sky. The two-lane freeway, if you can call it that, was in disrepair, a slalom course of ruts and potholes. I will never forget how the road rolled like sea swells on the ocean under the squishy suspension of the taxi.

I had done a bit of traveling in my life, but this was my first time in Europe, and more significantly, my first time in the former Communist world. The images flashed past me. Each new sight made me feel increasingly uneasy and reminded me that everything had changed.

As we sailed toward the city limits, I watched the simply dressed Albanians walking along where cars were designed to drive. I saw fields of greenhouses, now free of glass and abandoned, like huge metal birdcages. We passed small huddles of government police, chatting and smoking, seemingly without cares or responsibility.

Months before, when I looked at a global map, Albania seemed much like my Oregon home. Placed with the sea to the west, it was full of mountains, rivers, and valleys. When I traced my finger along the horizontal lines on the globe, I was delighted to find that both places shared a surprisingly similar distance from the equator.

In light of these kinships, the images out my window could not have been more disappointing. My eyes saw no trees. At home in Oregon, trees had always been my constant companions. Yet here, they were gone. Who could have taken all the trees?

In the trees' place now stood pillbox bunkers. There were thousands upon thousands of them, hideous concrete bulbs, each one the size and shape of a cartoon igloo. I could only guess that these pillboxes were built to communicate defense and strength. They were what they were: a psychological solution to a military problem, powerful in appearance but dubious in effect.

As I stared at the Albanian landscape, I imaged that someone had taken a long, dull razor across her face, scraping away all growth and leaving only an irritated, pimpled surface behind.

———

I was twenty-one. Just a few weeks out of university, filled with religious fervor and the sort of self-important idealism that accompanies a theatrical heart.

Nine months before that ride from the Albania airport, I sat in Portland with my friend Cheryl. Cheryl had recently returned from a year in Romania, and I was interrogating her about life outside the United States.

"I want to live overseas," I told her. "What can you teach me?"

Cheryl spoke freely. Though she clearly had a deep affection for Romania, I remember that she couldn't stop talking about Albania. "I can't believe it; Albania is finally opening up," she said. Her voice bounced as she talked about it. "After fifty years of being totally hidden behind the Communist wall, it is now opening up. Albania is not like the rest of Eastern Europe. Under Communism you could visit Romania or even Russia if you really wanted. Not Albania. For five decades no one has been in or out. No one has even seen what goes on there. And"—she paused for impact—"it's Muslim."

She let that last statement just hang in the air.

"I would give anything to be on that first team that goes in." Cheryl's eyes twinkled when she spoke. I loved that about her.

When our conversation ended, I tried to imagine myself going to Albania. I closed my eyes to picture it, but what I saw was nothing but a blank canvas. Albania to me was only a single fill-in-the-blank answer on an eighth-grade geography test, nothing more. So I put the whole idea out of my mind.

———————

A few months later graduation was drawing near and I was starting to get desperate. Soon I would be armed with a communications degree from my state university. In the place of traditional career aspirations, I had a longing to live outside my cloistered Oregon home. I needed a travel agent more than a career counselor.

One afternoon in March, drunk with curiosity, I dialed an international Christian agency. I asked for someone in international placement. Within moments, a kind-sounding lady came on the phone and asked how she could help.

I didn't even think to introduce myself. I told her that I was finishing college and looking to move outside of the United States. I didn't want to take much of her time. I had just one question to ask her. "Where is the greatest need in the world *right now?*"

"Excuse me?" she asked.

I said it again, emphasizing each word. "Where is the greatest need in the world right now?"

Understandably, she was caught off guard by my question. For a moment there was only silence. Then she spoke. "That is a difficult question. I am not sure what you mean by 'greatest need.'" She seemed to be processing her thoughts out loud. "I did just get out of a meeting, though . . . I don't know if you know this, but Albania just opened up, and we have a wonderful chance to send a team there. We were hoping to send some people in just a few months. The only problem is no one seems to want to go, at least not right now. I mean . . . that is not exactly true. We actually have six applicants. Thing is, only females have applied."

Now, I would like to say that the idea of traveling somewhere dangerous, the sole male in the company of six women, was not the appeal that pushed me to say yes. But such a thought might be too much to ask of a twenty-one-year-old daydreaming virgin.

The lady on the other end of the phone continued. "It is a once-in-a-lifetime opportunity, if only we could get a full team to go."

That was all I needed to know. Without hesitation I said, "I'll go."

"What did you say?" she asked.

I said, "That's it. *That* is why I called. Sign me up."

I could tell by the tone in her voice that I had done something wrong. Her words were full of compassion. "I'm sorry. I don't think you understand." I think she was trying to use small words for my benefit. Her voice became even sweeter as she continued. "That is not the way these things work. You don't just say where you want to go . . . at least not like that. These things take time, you see . . . Oh my . . . let me try to explain."

I was as compliant as I was idealistic. I just listened, giving her an "uh-huh" after every phrase.

She continued, "It works like this. You need to pray first. You might need to pray for a long time. You then need to seek advice from people who know you and love you. Finally, you are going to have to go through a long application process."

With a new sense of enlightenment, I replied, "Of course; all that makes perfect sense. Thank you for explaining all this to me. But as long as you have me on the phone, you may just want to go ahead and put me down for Albania." Without waiting for her to respond, I started to spell my name and asked if she had written it down correctly.

And that's how it began. The imagination of my friend Cheryl, a curiosity-fueled phone call, and those magical words: "a once-in-a-lifetime opportunity."

My course was set, and I never considered looking back.

———

I started to read more and found out that Albania was alone and isolated in a forgotten corner of Europe. She had been isolated geographically by mountains and a sea. She had been isolated politically by fifty years of particularly autocratic Stalinist socialism. She had been isolated historically by her unique Muslim roots. That sense of loneliness drew me to her.

On the other hand, Albania felt like a *Casablanca* movie poster, emanating both mystery and discovery. My family had been in Oregon for generations. We were old pioneers, and Albania felt like another chance to enter the truly unknown. This adventure required my full devotion, and my pioneer programming pushed me to self-reliance, individualism, and risk.

Also, like the American pioneers, I felt that Albania was a land that needed to be conquered. For me, Muslims were the purest example of my religious enemy, and with love as my weapon, I was ready to be sent into the enemy's land.

━━━━━

The taxi left the pimpled countryside and followed the boulevard into Tirana's city center. We took a quick lap around the square. In rapid succession we passed the National Museum, the Palace of Culture, the city's central mosque, a towering iron statue of Albania's medieval national hero, and the National Bank. We continued east, onto a smaller arterial road. Buildings and boulevards bounded by.

At the next broad intersection, we stopped to wait our turn. The taxi driver could have honked all day, but his chance to cross would not come until all the larger vehicles had bullied through first.

Out the window to my right, there was a three-story-deep hole, just sitting there, purposeless, filling half a city block. I later learned that it was a long-abandoned building project that was supposed to house a modern high-rise hotel. The hotel was never built, but the hole remained, a monument to progress lost.

Off the main drag, the taxi turned into a tight and winding neighborhood, over dirt and cobblestone. A right, then a left and another right; I tried to memorize the path so I could find my way back out should I need to escape. No such luck. I was quickly lost.

When we finally stopped, we were in a small cul-de-sac, large enough to park a dozen cars. All around were high walls, which was typical of private neighborhoods in that area of the city. At the back of the lot was an elegant, Mediterranean-looking home, rising above the wall. I hoped it would be *my* new home. It was not.

Instead I was directed to a small wooden gate to my left. It was set inside a rough-hewn frame, embedded in a tall brick wall. The wood was black, and the latch was from a different age. The gate was no larger than the door on a wardrobe.

I stepped through the wardrobe-gate and found a narrow flag path, which opened a dozen meters down into a small courtyard. I later learned that this block was the historical plot of a single clan. Over the generations the plot had been divided and divided again to create homes for various cousins. My landlords lived in one of the central homes, now wedged between half a dozen other family houses. The courtyard was six meters by fifteen, with their simple home filling the back end. There were grapevines atop the three-meter-tall surround. A single tangerine tree, like something out of a Frost poem, climbed out of the courtyard's only small patch of dirt.

The house was a simple box. The bottom floor held just two rooms, each with a double wood-framed window opening to the courtyard. This floor was sunken slightly. As I looked up, I saw that the upper floor also appeared to have two simple rooms, accessed by a narrow balcony walkway running the width of the home.

The time had come to meet my landlords.

Before arriving, I had been told surprisingly little about my actual life in Albania. I believed that I would be staying in something of a boardinghouse, run by a Muslim family, the sort of place where you pay for a room but live fairly independently. That vision of independence was very comforting to me. It meant I could control my life. It also meant I could keep a safe distance from my Muslim landlords. The reality, however, was quite different.

Anticipation left my heart pounding. It was the moment that I had been dreading for months. *What will I say to these Muslim people?* I thought. *How will we live together? What will this life be like?*

I had tried to imagine why this Muslim family would allow a Christian missionary to live in their home. *Was I their mission as much as they were mine?*

No more time for questions. The moment of truth had come,

and I was too tired to worry about it anymore. I hoped our introductions would be brief, the sorts that my parents had instilled in me when meeting guests at a function: "Hello. So nice to meet you. Thank you for your hospitality." Then I could slip away to my room and disappear for the night . . . or a week.

No such luck.

My landlords stood together in front of the house. There were five of them. Most prominent were the two men, Ani and Ari. Both were a few inches shorter than I, with strong, thin builds. Ani had short-cropped hair, and judging by how he carried himself, he was the head of the household. Ari's hair was longer, and though also a grown man, he was more playful in appearance. Ariana was Ani's wife, lovely and soft-spoken. Ridi was their young son, only two years old. Finally, there was Fidnet. The old woman held herself back, eclipsed between the shoulders of her two sons. She was bent slightly, and a hard life had left her appearing much, much older than her actual age. Her head and hands shook just a bit, and her face was filled with a soft smile. She was as beautiful as anything I had ever seen.

We were all quickly introduced.

They laughed at the sight of me. There were a few other Americans also staying in their home. I was the tallest of the group, but the youngest in age. The family immediately christened me "Toni i vogel," which means "Little Toni." They each laughed as they said it, amused by the irony: little in age but not little in size.

With the help of friends, the language barrier was crossed and the basics of the home were explained. The bathroom was in the courtyard; a tool shed–sized concrete enclosure with a porcelain hole in the floor and a small sink. Near me, in the corner, were a few pots and cooking implements. It appeared the cooking was also done outside.

Inside the house, it was as I had assessed: two rooms below and two above. I took a quick account, trying to make the numbers work: a family of five and four full-sized foreign males. That means nine people in four rooms. Oh boy.

We climbed the tiled stairwell to the second-floor balcony. The tiles were white, yellow, and green, and immaculately kept. In fact, everything was perfectly clean and organized. To maneuver along the narrow balcony, between the iron railing and wall, I had to hold my bag in front of me while ducking slightly; the leaves of the grapevines hanging above my head brushed my face.

I was to stay in the second room. I removed my shoes and stepped in to absorb my space. A rich Turkish rug covered the floor. I was pointed to a divan-style bed and a freestanding closet for my things. Everything looked lovely. I am not the sort of person who needs much to feel comfortable. I wanted to communicate my thankfulness. Tragically, like an American cliché, I did not speak even one word of the Albanian language. So, what could I do? With a dramatic flourish I spread myself across my bed, with my hands tucked behind my head, a broad smile on my face and my legs crossed. I wanted to announce to everyone that I was "here to stay."

They all laughed. They laughed in part at my playfulness, but it was also because my feet hung a good four inches off the end of the bed. I looked up to see Ariana. She alone was not laughing. Her brow was furrowed. Everything was not perfect. She immediately brainstormed a solution to this hospitality conundrum. By the next day there would be a simple extension added to the end of my bed. This woman, whose home I was invading, not only accommodated me, but it was soon clear that she actually cared for my comfort and well-being.

Sinking into the metal springs, I closed my eyes. I hoped everyone would quietly slip out and leave me. I wanted to drift to sleep, happy to dream in my travel clothes.

The contentment lasted only a moment. No one left the room. Opening one eye, I looked around. They were giving me the "look."

It is the same look my mom used to give me when it was time to leave the toy store or the look my teacher would give me when I needed to get back to class. It was clear. I needed to get up.

I forced my frame up from bed. Outside, I found the hazy blue of dust.

One of the lower rooms served as the gathering space and dining room. We sat around the table. Bread, jam, cheese, salami, and apples were all laid out for a proper Mediterranean supper. It was our first foray into sharing life together. With a bit of language help, but still a very limited shared vocabulary, we began to get to know one another. We talked and we talked. Time was lost. We were able to get through basic details, like age, family, and where we came from. It is amazing what you can communicate with ten fingers and an adventurous face. Everyone was patient with the slow understanding. The laughter was generous.

Deep into the time of darkness, I was finally released to go to bed. With my last moments of consciousness, I thought about where I had landed. These people were not scary; they were a delight. In just a few hours I had experienced the very first aroma of a few life-altering truths.

This was not a boardinghouse; this was going to be my home.

These were not my landlords; they would soon become my family.

These were not "Muslims"; they were . . . well, that one is a bit more complicated.

2

GOSPEL

I WAS RAISED IN A TWO-TEAM WORLD. IT WAS NOT AS BLATANT as a white-versus-black world or a rich-versus-poor world, but it was a two-team world all the same. My two-team world was one of the spiritual haves and have-nots. (The "haves" were Christians. The "have-nots" were everybody else.) Thankfully, I was a have.

I have many memories of Sunday school growing up. In many ways, you could say that Sunday school was my second home. There were few other places where I spent more time. There were few other places where I felt more accepted or more in control.

I was a religious kid living in an incredibly nonreligious town. I was a scrawny kid, and not a particularly bright one, living in a culture of privilege, a city full of success and physical prowess. I didn't fit in.

Church, on the other hand, didn't ask me to spell correctly, dress cool, jump high, or run fast (It was one place where I could just be.) I am still thankful for that.

I can remember one Sunday morning. It was much like any Sunday morning in the mid to late eighties. My pastor—handsome, charismatic, and smart—was explaining the evil of other religions and the need to maintain Christian purity. "Other beliefs are dangerous," he said. "They are not to be played with; they are not to be entertained. Anyone who has been seduced by such beliefs is lost, painfully lost.

"Do not be yoked together with unbelievers," he warned, quoting his Bible. "Don't get too close to those who are not Christians. When you do meet someone who is lost, do what you can to share with them about Jesus, and bring them with you to church. Remember that you have the truth and they do not."

———

It didn't take long for me to adore Fidnet, my Albanian grandmother. What's not to like?

Fidnet was generous with her smiles. She seemed to work all day long around the house. I never heard her complain. I rarely saw her do something solely for herself. She was diminutive, ever puttering around in her plastic house slippers, rolled stockings, and a simple, worn skirt and buttoned sweater. There was nothing—nothing—about her that one would consider threatening. She was both my dearest companion and my archenemy.

Each morning I woke to the haunting sound of the Muslim call to prayer echoing from the city center, bouncing and bounding across the housetops. The call was tenacious and unyielding as a guard dog. The first moment of every day, I was told in whose country I lived. I was reminded in whose territory I had slept.

I rose from bed quickly back in those days, dressed in whatever was near at hand, and shuffled out on the balcony and down the stairs. The first stop was our outdoor bathroom. I was always thankful to find a dry morning.

Most mornings I would see Fidnet in the courtyard. She was often working a handheld broom of bound straw across the concrete courtyard, making sure that not a single leaf cluttered the gray surface. As she swept, I could hear her humming to herself along with the aching song from the city mosque. I rarely saw her on her knees, praying toward the east, like the Muslims in the movies; but like Brother Lawrence, she would sing and pray along with the rhythm of her broom.

Our early morning exchange would go something like this: She would not see me until I was practically standing next to her. And once she did, she would blush and wave me off. She would half apologize, half scold me for catching her in her private song.

Sometimes I felt ashamed that I had disturbed her. Usually, though, I took the opportunity to embarrass her further by telling her how beautiful her singing was and how she should sing louder for all the neighbors to hear. She pretended to hate this, but I often caught her shy smile.

We went on like this most days. She would take care of me, and I would make her laugh. It was our unspoken agreement. I would find little ways to embarrass her, and she would utilize every Albanian superstition to annoy the crap out of me. Superstitions were just her way. I should have accepted them as such, but they grated against my spiritual pragmatism.

When I say *superstition*, this is what I mean:

If I took a book into the courtyard and tried to sit on the ground, leaning up against a wall, Fidnet would come around the corner, wailing at me. She would say, "Get up! Get up!" Then she would go on and on, using words I didn't much recognize, but her rant appeared to have something to do with the cool concrete freezing my testicles.

Or when I'd come in from playing basketball, soaking in my own sweat, I would, like any reasonable human being, pour myself a tall glass of water. But if Fidnet caught me, I would endure a tirade. "Don't drink that much water!" "Don't drink it so fast!" "Don't drink water that is cold!" I tried to respond in the power of demonstrative communication I had learned in Albania (they talk with their faces, their arms, their hands, their hips; communication is a whole-body experience): I would flap my arms around and say, "Why? Why can't I drink the water?" And she would respond with equal gesticulation, ranting some sort of craziness about my "fire going out." As she said *fire*, she would point to the center of her chest.

It was exhausting.

One particular day I came home, tired and sweaty. I slipped carefully into the house to sneak a glass of water. That's right; I had to sneak *a glass of water*. I felt like a teenager trying to steal vodka from his dad's liquor cabinet (not that I would know anything about that).

My contraband refreshment was clear and perfect in my hand. My mouth watered at the very sight of it, the moisture beading up on the glass surface.

Then she appeared. She came in swinging her arms and yelling at me like a deranged hobbit.

I couldn't take it anymore. I snapped.

I turned to meet her and stared her down. I raised the glass up. I held it to the far side of my mouth, against my cheek so I could maintain absolute eye contact with her. Through the very corner of my mouth I poured the clear contents, chugging it down. I was sure to vocalize each gulp. Gulp! Gulp! I wanted her to know: This! Right now. This is the moment that my fire goes out.

The old woman stopped cold, absorbing every ounce of my insolence. Her eyes were round. Her ever-smile was gone. With her head slowly shaking back and forth, she gave out a long, slow "Buh buh buh buh." This repeated sound may not seem like much to you, but when a person of honor in Albania releases a heavy load of "Buh buh buh buh," there is nothing more to be said. No defense can be made. No retort will be heard. She turned from me, dismissing me with a two-hand flap, as if she were erasing my face from existence. Then she walked away.

Any sense of victory disappeared as she did. My arrogance was replaced by shame.

Fidnet was not the sort to hold a grudge, at least not with me, and by the end of the day, we were back to our old hijinks.

———

One morning, several months into my time in Albania, I woke feeling something I had not yet felt in my time away from home: loneliness. More than loneliness, it was a deep, gnawing sort of loneliness. It had nothing to do with not having people around. There were plenty of people around. It had nothing to do with some sort of boredom or lack of purpose. My life was full of purpose.

My problem was, the people around me were not the people I really wanted around me. I could see the faces of those *missing* people in my head. If I closed my eyes, I could almost feel them, sitting across the room, just beyond my reach. I was lonely without them.

Lonely and *alone* are the scariest words in the English language.

I didn't get up with the call to prayer that morning. I stayed in bed. When I did dig myself out, then trudged down the stairs, Fidnet met me in the courtyard. She looked me over. In her long-tested wisdom, she did not need my words for her to know the whole of my story. She said nothing to draw attention to me. She just quietly asked me to "Come along." As I ducked into the house's lower level, she patted me gently and said what she knew would bring me a small slice of comfort, "Bread with egg," the Albanian phrase for French toast. My face tried a small smile. It didn't take.

She cooked my bread with egg without looking at me. She hummed a bit to herself. When done, she handed the sizzling browned bread to me, and I thanked her. She allowed me to eat in silence for a few minutes. When the time was right, she came over. She spoke in simple Albanian phrases so I could understand.

"O Little Tony, why are you so much sad? Do you have missing for your family?"

Her words were comforting. It was so wonderful to have someone who cared about me, who seemed to understand without my having to explain. These few words were what I needed to hear. I just wish she had stopped at that and said no more.

Unfortunately, she went on.

"God is good. God is good to you. With God you are not alone. God has given you much. You need to have faith."

Instantly I was incensed. *Who is* she *to tell* me *that I need faith?* I thought. She could be grandmotherly anytime she wanted. But to give me advice on faith was not something I could swallow.

I abruptly thanked her for the breakfast and stomped out.

———

Back on the campus of the National University, I had a friend named Geni. He was from a city in the south. I met him during my first week in the country. I think he was my first *real* Albanian friend.

The first time I met him, I am sure that I looked as wide-eyed and afraid as a child at his first recital. He caught me in the dormitory stairwell, totally lost, and immediately and unceremoniously told me to come to his room.

Geni was not an impressive fellow, with dishwater-blond hair and a thin mustache. Jesus once referred to one of his disciples as being a "man in whom there is no deceit," and I imagine he would have said the same about Geni. He had a dry and straightforward style to him. At first I thought he was annoyed with me; then I learned it was just his way.

Once inside his room, his first question, direct and arrow-true, was, "Are you a Christian?"

I told him I was and asked him how he could have possibly known that. His reply was as direct as his nature: "Why else would someone like you be *here?*"

He then told me that he was a Christian as well.

Over the months, Geni and I would spend time together often and in time became quite close. I eventually met his entire family, spent holidays with them, and our stories became indelibly intertwined.

In the same week as my bout with loneliness and indignation toward Fidnet, Geni and I met at a quiet café.

The waiter placed between us two cups of Turkish coffee, a thick layer of grounds floating on top of each. Have you ever tried to drink Turkish coffee? I had been told to drink the coffee through my teeth to filter the grounds, but I hated the thoughts of all that grit stuck in my teeth and in the corners of my gums. Instead, I devised a plan of my own. I would extend my upper lip as far forward as possible and plunge it through the floating grounds to siphon the coffee below. It proved to be reasonably effective, except when the coffee was too hot, a lesson I learned the hard way.

My conversation with Geni quickly turned to faith, and specifically, our story of Christian discovery. He told me he had been following Jesus for about two years.

As soon as he said it, I was confused. The math didn't work. Two years before would have been just around the time of the revolution. My understanding was that there had been no—zero, really—Christian witness under the radical Communist dictatorship.

"Geni," I asked him, "how did you come to be a Christian so long ago?"

He went on to tell me an incredible story.

Geni was in the engineering school at the university. He had a great love of science. Through circumstances that I do not now recall, two years before he had managed to come upon a *Scientific American* magazine. He explained how much he treasured every page. The most significant article was on quasars. I am a science illiterate, so he took his time. It was clear that he wanted me to understand the details of his story. He explained to me that quasars are among the largest and most luminous objects we have ever discovered. "They are ultimately huge," he exclaimed.

"I could not stop thinking about quasars," Geni continued. He was no longer looking me in the eye, but was lost in the memory. "Compared to a quasar, our galaxy is nothing. It is only a piece of sand. Just a piece of sand." He rubbed his thumb and finger together to illustrate just how small that was. "Then if you compare our sun system to our galaxy, *it* is only a piece of sand. It is a piece of sand inside a piece of sand. Then you have planet Earth. Earth is only a piece of sand in our sun system. That is a piece of sand inside a piece of sand inside a piece of sand." This mathematical drama was clearly inspiring to him. He continued. "Albania is a very small country. Albania is only a piece of sand on the earth and . . ." Geni now looked me straight in the eye. "Tony, I am only a piece of sand inside my piece-of-sand country. I ask you, what could be more insignificant than me? Can you see that I am the smallest piece of nothing in the whole universe?"

Geni's words were so simple; his logic was so perfect. I was now the one lost in his telescoping imagination.

"But Tony," he went on, "the words of the magazine were speaking to me so clearly. They reminded me that I am in fact significant. How could this be? God was speaking to me through the pages of my magazine. He was telling me that even though I was ultimately small, I was also valuable, and I knew God was right."

I was mesmerized.

He did not stop. "I had heard whispered stories of Jesus. So I decided to respond to the God who spoke to me through the quasar article. I decided to be a Christian."

"And all this because you read a *Scientific American* magazine?"

"Yes," he said. "God spoke to me there."

This was one of the greatest stories I had ever heard. It made my heart leap. It filled me with worship. It made me want to dance like King David.

That evening I hurried back to the house. I met several of my missionary friends and recounted the tale of faith that I had heard. "How wonderful and creative God is that he would speak so clearly through *Scientific American*."

One of my friends was very skeptical. "I don't know if that's even possible," she said with acrimony. "*Scientific American* hates Christianity. It teaches evolution and humanism. It teaches science over faith. That magazine hates God."

"I don't know about all that," I said, "but it appears that at least one article about quasars teaches people to believe in God." I laughed as I said it.

She didn't think it was funny.

———

Before I went to bed, I saw Fidnet again. She asked me if I was still sad. I told her no. It was the truth.

She said she was happy to hear that. She patted me gently on the elbow and said, "Sweet sleep."

As she toddled into the house, I thought about my sweet Fidnet. She was so kind to me. No one could deny her character and love. And yet I had been so dark toward her that morning when she spoke for God.

Then I thought about Geni and his encounter with God through a science magazine. Why was it so easy for me to accept God's voice through a magazine? Why was it so difficult for me to accept his voice through an elderly woman who I knew loved me and was full of virtue? I searched my heart.

In the end, there was only one answer. I could not get over the fact that she was a Muslim.

———

I was raised in a two-team world. It was not as blatant as a white-versus-black world or a rich-versus-poor world, but it was a two-team world all the same. My two-team world was one of the spiritual haves and have-nots. The "haves" were Christians. The "have-nots" were everybody else.

3

HOLY KISS

ANI TOOK TWO QUICK STRIDES AND HE WAS STANDING NEARLY against me. This was not the first time I would be startled by the scant size of the Albanian spatial bubble. He took my hand in his. His face shone in the early evening light with a huge smile and sparkling eyes. His head bobbled slightly as he talked. He spun several sentences of what sounded only of gibberish to my shamefully unseasoned American ears.

Then it happened.

Startling, to say the least.

If you had asked, I would have said that it was impossible for Ani and me to stand any closer.

I was wrong. So very wrong.

Gripping my hand and forearm, Ani pulled me closer. Then he pulled me closer still. He was not a large man, but I could not deny his strength. Then, with celebrative force, he kissed me square on the cheek. Remembering it now, my memories move in slow motion. He slowly released, pulling away only so slightly. I can imagine the look on my face. In shock, I watched his face pass in front of mine, only millimeters separating our noses, mouths, and chins. His face was all smile and bobble. Then he kissed my other cheek, just as hospitably as he did the first.

Only then did he step away. There was still moisture on the soft center of each of my cheeks.

That night, as I lay in the dark on my divan-style bed, staring at the ceiling, I could still feel the shape of his lips on each cheek.

This was one of my first experiences with one of my favorite men I have ever known.

———

Touch was stolen from me.

It was stolen from me by the American story. It was stolen from me by our puritanical religious roots, and by an entertainment culture that turns affection into sensuality. It was stolen from me by a thousand church scandals that have left pastors afraid to even talk to a parishioner behind closed doors. And it has been stolen from me by a generation of homophobia that calls all same-gender affection into question.

Society and religion have bedded together to relegate touch to either the sexual or the inappropriate, with little in between.

———

I had only been in country for a few months when I met Ilir and Genci. They had been best friends since childhood, and I imagine they will be for decades to come. That is the Albanian way.

They were a rugged duo from a small, outlying city. When I say *rugged*, I really mean rough, even a bit scary. When I first saw them in the dim corridor of their dormitory, I must admit I was instinctually on my guard. They both had dark eyes and black hair with weathered skin. Ilir was the slighter of the two, thin, with sunken cheeks and narrow eyes. Genci was broad. He had crazy hair and thick beard growth. Both wore leather coats covered with creases and cracks.

My first impression, judging them as hoodlums, was not without some merit. A few weeks after meeting them, I saw Ilir on Albanian national television. One of the charming practices of the Albanian police at the time was to place people suspected of crime in publicly displayed lineups. My guess is that the shame was used as a crime deterrent.

Ilir was never convicted; I don't know if he was even charged.

That first day, the day we became friends, I was just wandering through their dormitory. It was an average sort of day for me during those first months. My time was spent mostly with students. I was a young missionary, simply trying to make friends and searching for anyone who might want to talk about Jesus.

As soon as Ilir and Genci saw me, they erupted in hospitality. They dragged me from the hallway and through their door. It was a typical room on the Tirana campus. It was small, no larger than a prison cell. There was one missing pane in their window, crudely replaced by a piece of cardboard. A few other panes were cracked. Floor and walls were simple concrete. A single bare bulb suspended from a serpentine wire rocked in the middle of the room. A few pictures, pilfered from Western magazines, clung to the walls above their beds on either side. I guessed these pages had been taken from an airline magazine.

As was typical, the beds were the only things to sit on. A thin mattress lay across a metal hammock pulled taut across an iron frame. I dropped into the middle of the hammock with my shoulder blades and head against the chalky wall.

Ilir offered me a drink of Fanta from a plastic bottle. I said thank you but that I was fine.

He and Genci plopped onto the bed. They took a place on either side of me, dipping the metal hammock even lower. The other bed was only a meter away and lay empty, but they seemed more content to sit all together, the droop of the bed ensuring that we would remain bosom close.

I was still not sure what to make of these scruffy men. I wasn't sure I wanted them this close, their pungent aroma mixing with mine. By all indications, they could not have been more comfortable. Clearly they wanted to talk. I am not saying that there was any reason for concern, but I also knew that I was not going to do anything to upset them. I smiled to either side and tried to fully receive their physical offer of friendship.

After a while I asked if I could read them something about Jesus. They seemed unconcerned about the historical rift between their faith and mine. They seemed happy to just be together. So, I pulled out a small book.

I opened the pages.

Then, the most surprising thing happened.

Instinctively, Genci, sitting on my left, wrapped his arms around my arm, like a child, and laid his head upon my shoulder. His crazy hair brushed my chin and ear. He was ready to listen to whatever I might want to share.

At first Ilir scooted away a bit. I thought for a second that he might be the more reserved of the two.

I was wrong.

After judging the distance, Ilir leaned over, sliding his torso under my right arm and placing his head square in the middle of my chest. He placed his right hand carefully on my belly. He had secured the best view possible of my little book. As I read, he could feel the vibration of my voice through my chest. He could feel my lungs rise and contract.

And there we sat for the better part of the afternoon. We talked about Jesus. We talked about family. They shared with me their story. They told me about their dreams.

That year I started to read my Bible in a new way. I started to see touch everywhere, particularly in the Gospels: fathers embracing sons, secretive contact by a peasant woman, a disciple leaning on Jesus' bosom, hands washing and drying feet, heads anointed with oil. "Put your finger here; see my hands. Reach out your hand and put it into my side."

Could it be that touch has more to do with the Way of Jesus than what I had been taught?

When Jesus touched the leper, it transmitted the gospel of healing; I had known that since I was a boy.

But was the touch *itself* also a part of the gospel?

I began to see the leper story differently. The very act of touching was as much a miracle as the cleansing of his disease. Touch connected Jesus to the leper. Touch transmitted and affirmed humanity. Touch said, "You are not alone." Touch declared the leper's co-equality with all God-image beings. Ultimately, the touch of the Messiah erased a lifetime of isolation and rejection and a sentence to society's margins. Touch validated. Touch is love.

It has been so many years since I left that corner of the Muslim world, but I carry still the gift of my Albanian father, those scruffy friends, and my Middle Eastern messiah, who tactilely transmitted love.

These days, our faith family gathers for dinner every Sunday evening. As many as fifteen of us cram around our dining room table to share the meal called Agape. The food is always seasonal and delicious. Candles provide the light. The conversation lingers for hours.

Inevitably, if you look over, you will see Bobbin, all pierced and opinionated, sitting to my left. More often than not, he will have his arm around me or mine around him.

As I sit and enjoy Bobbin and our faith family all around, my mind starts to drift. There is a fear that rises up within me. I fear that touch, redeeming and healing touch, has just simply been lost.

———

Ironically, churches today seem to be driving themselves mad to compete with television, movies, and the Internet: supercharged sound systems, better bands, more charismatic characters. However, there are some things that the Web has not even come close to duplicating: a comforting touch on a shoulder, a sympathetic squeeze of the hand, a reassuring hug.

The very act of touching is a miracle. Touch connects us to the other. Touch transmits and affirms humanity. Touch welcomes. Touch says, "You are not alone." Touch declares the other's co-equality with all God-image beings. Ultimately, the holy touch of godly people can erase a lifetime of isolation, rejection, and daily sentencing to society's margins. Touch validates. Touch is love.

4

CRUSADE

ALBANIANS SOCIALIZE OVER DRINK.

They hold tiny glasses in their hands, full of one beverage or another (Turkish coffee, soda, beer, whiskey), and toast one another. They toast to happiness. They toast to long life.

In all of my travels, I have witnessed few cultures that bless one another as often and as effusively as I witnessed among the Albanian people. Albania has had a tough history. Maybe it takes that much tragedy to birth so much hope.

I once heard a story of the origin of this toasting tradition, specifically the part where glasses are clinked against each other. As it was explained to me, it began when one Norse tribe (or maybe it was Saxons; I can't remember) would meet together with neighboring tribes for a great feast. As the meal would commence, the tribal leaders would stand and toast one another. This was no country-club toast. They did not use delicate champagne flutes. They did not use moderation as they struck. Large, chunky steins of ale would crash into one another with impressive force. The goal of this goblet collision was to slosh your vessel's contents lavishly into your enemy's stein, and his into yours. It was an illustration of a shared event. It was a mixing of two distinct cultures.

The toast was also for protection. It was a guarantee that no one goblet or batch of ale had been poisoned. The sloshing assured that if one was poisoned, all were poisoned, thus creating mutually assured destruction.

———

During my high school years, and even into college, there was a great concern for having a pure faith, a faith that was uninfected by other beliefs. This sort of ideology sloshing was believed to be the worst form of faith betrayal.

To protect us from these Benedict Arnold ways, we were armed with ominous books, like *Kingdom of the Cults* and *Scaling the Secular City.*

I can remember my pastor back home standing high on the stage in his podium tower. There was a tiered choir loft behind him, full of red robes, and behind the paneled wall lay a secret baptism tub. The stage stretched the width of the old church, and my pastor was the unquestioned sage. He was handsome and the very look of wisdom. He always wore a suit and had perfectly groomed hair. I remember that he would wear his belt buckle pushed over to his hip, so all you could see was a seamless band of leather through his coat.

He warned us all, "Beware of the cults. They are not from God. They demand you submit to their leaders. In some ways they may look like Christianity, but they add other beliefs and allegiances not found in the Bible. Follow Jesus and Jesus alone."

I know he was talking to the entire sanctuary, but it felt like he was speaking only to me. He used a word that I had not heard before: *syncretism.* The very sound of it scared me. It meant mixing your beliefs with another belief system. "Cults," he said, "come from syncretism, from those who would betray the pure Christian faith."

Did you just feel a chilly sensation? I know I did.

He went on to explain that cults were marked by three distinct factors. "You will know cults by these three things. They are marked by dogmatic ideologies most often incorporating Christian language. They have authoritative structures, often led by charismatic personalities. And finally, they demand a passionate and emotional loyalty."

I loved my pastor and I knew that he would never do anything to hurt me. Still, his words scared me. I was afraid of my own limited capacity to believe. I had secret doubts. I was very careful. I kept the doubts locked deep inside my shadow self, in a place reserved for my many betrayals to God. Some of them had been there since childhood, and some, I feared, could unravel the entire fabric of my faith.

I was also afraid of the consequences that came with betrayal. I had watched the once-strong spiritual students, the "special" ones. They had at one time been given stage and microphone because they could exude confidence and devotion to their faith. They were the poster children, at least until they unexpectedly began the process of betrayal. It happened so often that we had a term for it. We called it "falling away." Falling away meant that they had thoughts of their own about their faith. These new thoughts led to new beliefs. At first these students were simply no longer offered the microphone. In time, as they continued in their ideological wandering, they slowly migrated from the front row to the edges of the room. Eventually they slipped unceremoniously out the door. After they were gone, we would often ask each other about them, speaking of them in hushed tones, as if they had died. We would promise each other that we would pray for them to return to a true faith.

I would do anything to avoid the club of the compromised, the cult of sloshed beliefs.

———

Genci, Ilir, and I were friends over a four-month period. They were charming and loyal and fun-loving. They had a great freedom about them. To them, any topic was a free game, and each conversation was a playground. They gave themselves freely and openly. They were the most refreshing of friends. I wish our friendship could have lasted longer, but in time, like many of their countrymen, they fled across the border in search of jobs and the promise of a better life.

They left without good-byes.

A couple months into our friendship, we talked for long hours in their room. We sat in their stretched metal hammock beds. Some days I needed a break from the intensity of the missionary life. On this day my friends gave me just the break I needed. Or so I thought.

It began as Genci asked me a bit about U.S. history, specifically, our story of independence. He was curious to hear my take on revolution and the rights of people to declare their own freedom as Albania had just a handful of months before.

We discussed honor and justice. We discussed oppression. We discussed violence as a tool of change. We shared stories of insurrection. We talked about the strong versus the weak.

They also wanted to know how I felt about being a citizen of the most powerful country in the world. It was fun for me. I got to talk about my country. I got to be the smart guy. My story was connected to a nation of success. My people were winners. I got to feel as if I was enlightened. Enlightenment is intoxicating.

As often happened, our conversation eventually turned to the topic of faith. They had questions. I was the expert witness, and these two Muslim men were playing the role of interviewer. I enjoyed it. They were firing questions at me, and I was doing my best to answer.

"How can you believe in Christianity when the Trinity makes no sense?"

"How can you believe in many gods? The Koran says that God is one."

"How can you believe the Bible when it is so full of mistakes?"

These questions were very typical in that season in Albania. With the new freedoms and an open border, many well-funded Muslim institutes saw Albania as an important European ally with a faith that needed to be supported and, as possible, strengthened. Dozens of new mosques were under construction all over the country. There were also extensive education strategies.

One such strategy was fueled by an Islamic scholar named Ahmed Deedat. Crates of books with ominous titles like *101 Contradictions in the Bible* were dumped around campus and on street corners for anyone to take, free of charge. It was an almost daily experience to find one of these blue-covered books in a student's room.

I had well-practiced answers to each of my friends' questions. I had answered them dozens of times. My answers were not intended to "win" the debate. I wanted to satisfy their intellect and curiosity. I wanted to continue the dance.

Then came an unexpected turn in their examination. It was a question for which I was *not* prepared. Ilir asked me, "How do you feel about the invasion of Muslim Kuwait and Iraq by a Christian USA?"

Any feeling of enlightenment or of being in control suddenly evaporated. I was on my heels and tried to answer him as best as I could: "It was the natural response of a superpower when there is injustice in the world. The Kuwaiti people had been wrongly invaded by Iraq, and the U.S. went there to set things right."

"And for oil," Ilir added quickly.

"Noooooo," I responded. I was surprised by his counterpunch. I tried to explain. "The oil issue is separate. The invasion was just about doing the right thing." This conversation was not so fun anymore, and I was getting annoyed and a little agitated.

"Sure, sure," he said. "In many ways Iraq was wrong. I agree with you there. But the USA would not have gone there and spent all that money if there wasn't all that oil."

"No!" I was officially angry. "That is not how it happened at all. Where did you hear these things?"

Both Ilir and Genci at this point sat up straight, and their eyes were all glistening with enjoyment. They started to talk more and more with their hands as well as with words. As in many cultures in the Mediterranean world, a conversation isn't *really* a conversation until someone starts to yell. Most often I was the soft-spoken one, while my Albanian friends got excited, but not this time. I was the one yelling. And this conversation was just getting started.

"Okay, what will your government do to help the people of Chechnya?"

Chechnya! What does Chechnya have to do with anything? I thought.

Ilir continued to press. "What will your country do when Chechnya needs your help?"

In the wake of the dismantling of the Soviet Union, Chechnya declared its independence without Russian permission. The saber rattling had already begun, and the future of Chechnya was predicted to be bloody. A Russian invasion a year and a half later would prove Ilir's fears to be prophetic.

"Chechnya is also a Muslim people," Ilir continued. "Will your government also come to their aid if they are invaded by Russia, the way they came to the aid of people of Kuwait? Will they fight for justice in Chechnya as well?"

Truthfully, I knew nothing about Chechnya. But what did that matter? I felt they were totally off topic. I was angered by their insolence. Who were they to question my country's actions and policies? I blurted out, "How can I possibly know what my country is going to do?"

At this point all three of us were yelling; however, as I think back, Genci and Ilir might have had a slight smile on their faces as we spat back and forth. To them this was the simple joy of banter. There was no validation in the topic. I, on the other hand, was not smiling.

"Here is my point," Ilir goaded. "You claim your country uses its power for justice. If your country is truly for justice, then *you should know* what your government will do. You should be able to answer my question about Chechnya. But since the USA is also motivated by oil, you cannot know if they will care." As he connected all these thoughts, he did so with a flourish. His arms swung wide as he finished, as if to say, "Ta-da!" He was clearly pleased with his summation.

I was livid. *Who does this guy think he is? If the world were a chessboard, my country is the king, and his would not even be a pawn. Who is he to sit here and lecture me about what the U.S. should or should not do? Who is he to question events that have not even happened yet? Doesn't he know that Albania benefits from the generosity of the U.S.? Don't they know that their country is indebted to us? They should know their place.*

It was then that my friends realized that our banter was not fun anymore. It was not fun for me, and therefore they did not want to continue, at least not in that vein. As the tide of emotion started to wash out of the room, Genci caught my gaze. He knew I was still angry. His question was direct.

"Tony," he said, "have you noticed that you defend your country more than you defend your God?"

His question smacked my soul.

I have a friend named Jared. We met many years after my time in Albania, when he was a graduate student at Reed College. He and I

35

had a small business together after our shared time at Reed. He is a Unitarian. (I am sure there is a thick chapter in my copy of *Kingdom of the Cults* addressing his church.)

Jared is a man of character. I was honored to trust my life and career in partnership with him. We never made much money, but I never doubted my decision to be with my friend.

One day, Jared taught me an indelible truth. You see, Jared and I are both opinionated dudes who are used to being right. So, as you might guess, we were often at odds in our business. Sometimes we were downright dramatic in our diatribes.

On this particular day, I lost my temper with Jared. I lost it like I had that day with Genci and Ilir.

My agitation filled the room. Normally this would lead to a fight, but not this time. This time it was different.

Jared spoke carefully. He knew he needed to be very intentional with his words. He also knew that he was talking to himself as much as to me.

"Tony," he said, "I am aware in myself that there are these moments when the level of my emotions is incongruent with the significance of the situation."

Jared really talks like this. He is kind of a smarty-pants with a knack for using four-syllable words.

"Let me explain. There are times when a person is supposed to be angry, even out of control, like when someone you love is in danger. At those times one is supposed to freak out. Right?" He paused to allow the thought to sink in. "There are other times when *my* emotions spike, but the immediate events are not equal to the spike. When this happens, if I can take a breath and get a little perspective, I try to ask myself, 'Jared, what are you *really* upset about?' I think it is safe to say that if my emotions are incongruent to the circumstance, then those emotions must be fueled by something else." He searched my eyes for evidence that he was making some sort of sense.

"Tony." He directed his words at me. Each one sank into my soul. "Tony, your emotions right now seem incongruent to our circumstances. They must be about something else. What is really bothering you?"

As you can probably guess, his words stopped me in my tracks. I could not help but search my heart and mind to find out what was really going on. *What is happening? Why am I so mad?* I realized that there is a part of my heart that controls me even though most days I don't know it is there. I took a deep breath. It only took a couple of moments of sanity for me to see clearly. There *was* a deeper issue affecting me.

The truth was, our business had been failing for some time. And if I really searched my inside language, I would have to admit that I believed I was a failure. My identity was linked to my failing work. I was not getting the success I needed to feel validated. And I was taking that failure out on my friend.

———

Walking home from my argument with Genci and Ilir (and once again, I may have been the only one having an argument), I started to think about the conversation's escalation. The longer I thought, the less I was concerned about who was right and who was wrong. I was more and more concerned by how much the conversation had bothered me, by how agitated I had become. I was particularly concerned that I would even slander those dear men in the courtroom of my mind.

What was I to do with Genci's question, "Tony, have you noticed that you defend your country more than you defend your God?"

What was wrong with me?

On each side of the stage where my pastor had stood (the same stage with the podium, the choir loft, and the hidden baptismal), there was a flag. In that hallowed sanctuary of my church growing up, where my pastor warned me about infecting my faith, a Christian flag stood on one side of the stage, and an American flag stood on the other, equal in size and prominence.

What message did these flags subtly teach this small boy, Sunday after Sunday after Sunday? Had these two flags also been planted side by side in my soul? Had I succumbed to a cult, a sort that my pastor never imagined? He had taught me that a cult was marked by three factors: a dogmatic ideology incorporating Christian language, an authoritative structure led by charismatic figures, and a demand for emotional loyalty.

The more I thought about it, the more I knew that the mug of my faith and the mug of my nationalism had sloshed into each other with a poisoning effect.

5

DEVOTION

YOU WOULD HAVE THOUGHT WE HAD KNOWN EACH OTHER ALL
our lives.

We walked together, arm in arm. He was just a bit shorter than
me. My arm draped around his neck and hung down over his left
shoulder. His right arm wrapped around the small of my back, and
his hand hooked in the nape of my right elbow.

It was distilled friendship.

In time, life in Albania became more comfortable. Slowly, there
were a few more products in the markets. Electricity flowed a little
more consistently. And eventually some private businesses started
to sprout.

I still remember the day the first small pizza restaurant opened
near the Tirana campus. It was a nondescript, unmarked corner
shop along the Elbasan road. No larger than a small living room, it
had just three standing tables in the center and an institutional display case at the far end. Behind the case worked two to three women

NEIGHBORS AND WISE MEN

in thick aprons, white handkerchiefs over their hair. The floor was covered with cracked or missing tiles. The walls were blank.

It was reasonably clean. Thus ends the endorsement.

The pizza was prepared on large industrial cooking sheets and cut into rectangles the size of a large slice of bread. You didn't want to be given a piece from the center of the sheet because those were particularly soggy. They were not soggy like greasy soggy; they were more wet-sponge soggy. Greasy soggy could have been delectable in that happy-hour menu sort of way, but wet-sponge soggy was merely . . . squishy. On top of the soggy crust was a sparing layer of canned tomato sauce, and on top of that a chalky sort of cheese, sour in flavor. It was a kind of cheese that was fairly easy to find in the markets. The pizza came in two flavors: you could have chalky cheese flavor or, if you were willing to spend a little more, your slice could include a couple of small pieces of fleshy salami the color of a pencil eraser.

The eraser-salami flavor was my favorite.

From the first day it opened, it was lunch Camelot, the shining light, the restaurant set "high upon a hill." In a great illustration of existential relativity, I could describe it in no other way, except "yummy."

———

I will never forget the first day he walked into the no-name pizza joint. He was wearing a denim jacket with a leather collar, button-down shirt, jeans, and sneakers. He oozed charisma. Some may have thought him arrogant. I know I did.

He did not walk; he strutted. He moved around the restaurant like Paul Newman in *Cool Hand Luke*.

I watched him from the first moment he came through the door. He met a friend standing at the closest table. They greeted with a kiss on each cheek and spoke close in a tone that I could not hear in the crowded din. He moved quickly around the room's perimeter, greeting several more patrons.

I was standing at the table in the middle of the room. He circled me as he went about his business, greeting as if it were a cocktail party, always with his back to the center. Then he spun and faced me.

"Look here; we have an American guy." It was not a challenge. It was playful. He said it with a wide grin on his face. He slapped the back of his fingers against the palm of the other hand as he said it. "What is your name, American guy?"

"My name is Tony," I said dispassionately. I was not sure if I was being played for a fool, so I wanted to keep my cards close. There was a part of me that liked him immediately and wanted to be his friend. There was another part of me fueled by suspicion. I feared that I had just met my nemesis. But I guess that makes sense. In the comic books, the nemesis is often the best friend.

"What is *your* name?" I asked.

"My name?" He chuckled. "My name is Lulëzim." He paused for a second, and then he leaned forward ever so slightly and asked, "Can you say my name?"

As you can probably guess, this was a trap. And there was really no way for me to get out of it. The trap was simple. There are several letters and sounds in the Albanian language that do not exist in the English language, and some are nearly impossible for the American tongue to pronounce. His unusual name had two of these difficult sounds. The ë is a unique vowel sound, and the *l* provides particular problems because Albanian also has a double *l* and, of course, the single *l* itself is particularly awkward for an ignorant American tongue. To make matters worse, he spoke quickly.

"Llullizim," I replied.

"No, *Lulëzim*. Say it."

A person's name is a very important thing. It is a point of

honor. It is a symbol of identity, and I really wanted to get his right. "Llullizim."

"No! *Lulëzim*. Try again."

By this time the room went silent. Everyone was listening, and all I could do was try again: "Lullezim."

"No." This time he said it slower, like he was talking to a small child. "Luuulëëëzim." Then he said it one last time with a definitive hand motion to show just how easy it was. "Lulëzim."

"I am sorry. I just can't say it." Then I tried one more time. "Lullëzim." I managed to get closer on the vowels, but I still terribly missed the second *l*.

"Okay, okay." He let me off the hook, patting me on the shoulder. "Good try, good try. So tell me, Tony, why are you in Albania?"

"I am here . . . um . . ." Now I was flustered. I was so afraid of saying something wrong. I tried to keep a strong external, but the truth was, I was intimidated, and that hadn't happened often. Attempting to regain my dignity, I spit out, "I am a missionary."

"A missionary man." He guffawed as he said it. "Tony, are you a Christian?"

"Yes, I am."

"Well, I am a Muslim. I am a proud Muslim man," he said, then placed his closed hand over his heart.

His eyes set against mine. I didn't know what to say.

Then he broke his gaze and said, "Okay, American man Tony. Nice to meet you. Don't forget my name: Lulëzim, Lulëzim."

With that he left me. I was very relieved that he did. I was left alone with my soggy pizza with pencil-eraser salami.

Tirana, in many ways, is a small city. Over the next few months, I would bump into *him* every week or so.

Once, he called to me from across the road. The voice came over the top of a passing diesel tractor. I did not see him, but I could hear him. And I knew immediately who it was: my nemesis.

"Hey Tony! Tony! Missionary Tony from America."

I looked for him. Dreading it. Then I saw him. He was waving one arm back and forth above his head. I waved back. I did not speak.

"What is my name?" he yelled. "Say my name!" He laughed as he called out. The sidewalks were full of people, and he said it loud enough for all to hear.

I shrugged, and he just laughed louder. "Lulëzim!" Then he slapped his hands together dramatically and turned from me. He threw his arm over his friend's shoulder, and together they laughed and walked away.

He had an ability to steal my ego as easily as shooing a fly from a picnic.

Before that I had been walking pleasantly with a friend. Once Lulëzim was gone, she turned and asked me, "Who was that?"

I said, "Don't ask."

If you had told me that years later he would stand next to me in my wedding or that I would name my first son after him, I would have called you a dirty liar.

———

My encounters with Lulëzim were always variations of that day on the road. We would cross paths in the pizza restaurant, or I would see him around campus. He would taunt me. I would try to laugh it off. A couple of times I tried to talk to him about faith. He always insisted that he was a Muslim. He said it to indicate that the discussion was over.

This went on for about four months.

―――――――

One of my many responsibilities was helping to host visiting groups of missionary tourists. They would come for a few days or a few weeks. On one occasion I was a guide for a large group of college students from Ohio.

One of these tourists was named Matthew. He was not the sort of person you would take particular note of. He was as unimpressive as the pizza shop, the sort of man you might see at a party and later not remember he was even there. Matthew had come to Albania for just one reason. His heart had bent toward a young law student. It was something that could only be defined as a divine seed that had been placed in his heart for another person, someone who lived on the other side of the world from his safe Ohio home. He had prayed every day for a year for this single student. He came that March to Albania with one desire: to share the love of Jesus with this one young man.

Matthew had come for just one week.

On Thursday evening he tried to get me to talk to him. He obviously had something important he wanted to talk to me about, but every "short-termer" had something important to talk about, so I ignored him. He tried to tell me about this certain student he wanted me to meet. I dismissed his request. He implored that this student was special and if I would just . . . I told him I was sorry, but I had more important things to do. He told me his name was Luli. I had already tuned him out.

The next day, late in the afternoon, I was standing in a dimly lit student theater on the Tirana University campus. About an hour before, we had wrapped up a successful meeting attended by more than three hundred students. The gathering had been my responsibility, and I was steeping in the success.

I stood alone toward the front of the auditorium. There were just a few more details to complete, and I was looking forward to locking up. A heavy, orange electrical cord was half coiled around my left arm. My right arm danced the cord around my left in a figure-eight pattern.

I did not hear the door open as he entered at the back. I did not see his silhouette cast against the late-afternoon sunlight from the windowed foyer.

He was halfway down the left aisle before I realized I was no longer alone. I did not recognize him until he was immediately in front of me. He startled me. His countenance was different from anything I had seen from him before.

It was Lulëzim, the same Lulëzim from the pizza place and the busy street. He looked me over as if I were on the witness stand and he was the prosecutor. Then he spoke.

"Would you teach me the Bible?" He asked it just like that. He kept his voice low, but the words were unmistakable.

I did not know what to say.

He did not wait for me to respond. It was as if he had practiced what he intended to say. I took the cue and silently listened. "Matthew has been speaking with me all week. He said that he has been praying for me every day. Did you know that?"

"Yes, I did."

"Matthew has told me about Jesus. I want to learn the Bible, but I need help. I don't know what to read. I know you are busy. Wherever you can meet, whenever you are available, I will come to you."

I was both undone by his humility and doubtful of his sincerity.

I didn't know what to say. Part of me was tempted to shame him to avenge the embarrassments he had levied on me so many times. But how could I?

And so, in my own act of faith, I agreed to meet with him.

At first we met just once a week. Before long we were inseparable friends.

Lulëzim was voracious in reading the Bible. Though a full-time law student, he was determined and read the entire New Testament in less than a week. He found the story of Jesus inspiring. He found the words of Jesus worthy of following.

And I got to sit and watch it happen. It was an honor. Oh, and by the way, he quickly allowed me to call him Luli, a name I could pronounce correctly every time.

My temptation, because of my two-team programming, was to feel a sense of triumph over his change of heart. My team had won again. We had added another name to our role and taken a name from theirs. But in time, I had to repent of seeing my friend as some sort of Christian conquest. I was blinded by my belief that my team was "better," so much so that I could not see the cost. In time I realized what it took for a young, proud man to do what I had never, ever considered doing . . . following the path of faith wherever it might lead. Wherever! Luli was willing to do what I couldn't. Even if that meant immersing himself in an opposing religion. Even if that meant saturating his soul in the enemy's sacred texts.

Eventually, Luli became my teacher. He is the very example of courage. If we know a tree by its fruit, Luli was a tree with deep roots, planted by streams of water.

———

Now, many years later, it may surprise you to hear that Luli continues in the struggle of faith. He does not hide in the comfortable protection of religious labels. He is still following his path as best he can, come what may. While he is unapologetic about his love for Jesus, he would not refer to himself as a Christian.

I am proud to call myself Luli's friend. My friend Luli was raised under an atheistic Communist regime. As a young man he confidently proclaimed himself a Muslim. He comes from a Muslim city in northern Albania. He is the citizen of a predominantly Muslim country.

He is also a courageous man of faith. He is devoted to Jesus. And he is devoted to me.

———

If you had met us along the road in the years that followed, here is what you might have seen . . .

You would have thought we had known each other all our lives.

We walked together arm in arm. He was just a bit shorter than me. My arm draped around his neck and hung down over his left shoulder. His right arm wrapped around the small of my back and his hand hooked in the nape of my right elbow.

It is distilled friendship.

6

PASTOR

I WAS TRAINED TO TRUST TWO THINGS: MY BIBLE AND MY PASTOR.

Eventually the routine in Albania became downright comfortable. Even things like intermittent electricity, reading by candlelight, and warming my room with burning kerosene felt completely normal.

Books became my cinema. Storytelling became my television. The hour hike to campus was simply my commute. A herd of sheep was my traffic jam. If you don't know what it is to view Spam as a delicacy or Armed Forces Radio as a luxury, you haven't really lived.

And then there were the days when that glorious routine came to a screeching halt.

On the far side of the university campus stood Student City. It was composed of thirty dormitories stacked up a hillside. It was easy to imagine the dream that these dorms once represented: a hillside utopia complete with an elaborate center square, several spots for cafés and student clubs, even a student cinema. Seeing it now, the dream was left chipped, faded, and in disrepair.

As on most days, I passed the opulent U.S. embassy compound and then a large orphanage run by Baptist missionaries before turning to climb up into the dormitory complex. I passed sports yards where basketball backboards and bleachers once stood, but which now held only bent posts and rusting metal.

When I arrived at the Student City center square, there was an unusual happening. A crowd of a couple dozen students was gathered. Though I couldn't discern the attraction, I could see two tall woolen caps bobbing in the crowd's center.

I came closer. The students were solemn. They were intent. The wool hats sat on two regal and scholarly heads. One man had a full, white beard and was wearing a floor-length gray coat of natural fiber. The other man was younger, but equally refined; his beard and coat were both shorter and brown.

They appeared to be answering the students' questions. Each answer was a sermon, carefully and articulately presented. The men spoke in Arabic. A middle-aged man in a suit translated their words sentence by sentence into Albanian. I understood none of the Arabic and only some of the Albanian. The phrases were full of unfamiliar religious jargon. I could catch the gist, but not the substance of their words.

I turned and asked a student what was going on, and he explained, "These men are from a great Islamic institute. They have traveled here from Jordan and Saudi Arabia to teach us in the Muslim faith."

This was disturbing to me.

Any day of the week, you could find Muslim classes and services in the city, but this was different. These men carried so much authority. The crowd was growing by the minute. The two scholars held court deftly and persuasively.

I listened for half an hour. I tried to follow. Language learning has never been my strong suit. I found myself squinting my eyes, as if that would somehow empower my ears to understand. They spoke of the pillars of Islam, the character of Allah, and the need for absolute submission. They also extolled the greatness of Albania and how it was a bright light to the glory of the Islamic faith to Europe and, in fact, to the world.

I looked around at the students. They were rapt. Heads nodded in hypnotic agreement. It was clear they were not only being spiritually and intellectually stimulated; their nationalism was being inflamed. It was a powerful and euphoric combination.

———

Later that afternoon, on my way home from campus, I went to visit my pastor. I was concerned after those events in Student City, and I knew he would be able to help.

There were only a few churches in the city at this time. I went to one that had begun about the same time I had arrived. I loved my pastor. He was tall and handsome, like an action figure. He was also wonderfully insightful about the things of God. We had had many discussions where he opened my mind and spirit to things in faith I had never considered before.

I can remember one time we were walking along the lakeshore and talking about the beauty and creativity of God as a communicator. "Creation offers us unending lessons about God's character," he said. "Think of the moon. It has no light of its own, and yet it shines, reflecting the light of the sun. We are like the moon. God is the only source of true light, and yet he can reflect his light off anything he likes, even off a dead rock like me." He grinned as he called himself a "dead rock."

It was a poetic piece of truth that has stuck with me. Because of that conversation, I never looked at planets or trees or rivers the same again. Everything around me became a sermon.

On this particular day, I stopped by his office because I needed his advice. I had watched the battle for students' souls on campus that day, and by the look of things, our team was losing.

After explaining to him what I had witnessed, I said, "I think I need to do something about this. Somebody needs to stand up to these Muslim evangelizers. God needs somebody to stand for the truth." I was frustrated and definitely distraught.

"Well, that is a decision that you will have to make," he said. "Talk to me; what makes you think that you need to do this?"

In college I had been taught the spiritual concept we called "killing the giant." It was based on the boy David fighting the giant Goliath in the Old Testament. Essentially, you choose the scariest spiritual act you can think of (the giant) and go do it. It was the ultimate declaration of faith. Some of us would take a stand for Jesus in biology class. Others would share their faith with the most daunting people in their dormitory. I tried to explain the idea of "killing the giant" to my pastor and told him that these two false teachers represented a great test to my faith today. "They are the giant that I need to face."

"Okay," he answered, "so what are you going to do?"

"Confront them, I guess." But the more I thought about it, the more I had to admit that I did not have any idea what I would say.

My pastor pondered this.

"I don't know what you *can* say," he said finally. "I doubt anything you do will influence them. They will probably not even listen to you. However"—he rubbed his cheek with the fingertips of his left hand as he thought—"if you do get a chance to talk to them, I would confront them on the Trinity."

"Okay." That sounded like a good idea. "How do I do that?"

"I would start with this verse right here." At that, he opened his Bible and found a page near the back. He was about to read a verse from 1 John aloud, but before he could, he abruptly stopped himself. "I'm sorry. This may not be a good idea. Unfortunately, this verse is not in *your* Bible."

Excuse me? What did he just say? How could a verse be in his Bible that was not in my Bible? This was alarming . . . and it was about to get worse.

He tried to explain. "Your Bible is not really the true Bible, I'm sorry to say. I am sure this comes as something of a shock to you." He figured it was best to say it like ripping off a Band-Aid. "You can't really trust your translation of the Bible. For instance, there are verses, really essential verses, like this one I am trying to show you that your Bible doesn't have."

My head was swimming. What the heck was he talking about? I had been using this Bible for years. It was the version that my father read. It was the version that my mentor in college had taught me to read. And now my pastor was telling me that I can't trust it?

At this point, I had forgotten all about the Muslim evangelists, and apparently so had he. We had left scary-Muslim-scholar-land and were taking the bullet train to crazy-Bible-land. And my pastor was the train engineer.

"Your Bible was translated with a New Age agenda; mine was not."

I had always known that my pastor had a strong preference for his old-timey Bible translation. He had never been shy about that. But this was the first time he told me that my Bible was actually not trustworthy.

"For your own good you should probably read this." He grabbed a book off the corner of his desk. It looked like a Bible, thick and black, but instead of gilded lettering, this book had a large, red demon pictured on the front and was titled something like *The Evil*

Bible Translations, and below the red demon, my Bible was listed along with a dozen other popular Bible versions. To be honest, the book really freaked me out. Just holding it gave me the willies. For the first time, my pastor felt unsafe to me.

This was officially the worst day of my life. I learned I can't trust my Bible anymore. *And* my pastor didn't feel safe anymore either.

I gave him back his red-demon book and told him that I had to go.

He shook my hand and before he let go said, "Remember what we talked about."

I left.

I was alone on the street.

———

After a good night's sleep, I was able to put most of the previous day out of my mind. I was back in the routine. Up at six. Cup of coffee. Light the kerosene heater. Morning of reading and prayer. Then off to campus.

Without knowing why, I even had a bit of a spring in my step along my hour commute. I passed the embassy, the orphanage, and the dilapidated sports fields and began to climb the hill into Student City. I was lost in my thoughts and not much aware of anything around me. I think I was even humming a tune to myself.

I reached the first dormitories and the road joined another path, and both turned to the right. I turned and was jarred from my daydream. Just a few meters behind me, from the merging path, came the same bearded Muslim scholars. I just kept walking, stiff with surprise and fright, fighting the desire to look back. They were only a few strides behind me, so close I could hear their footsteps. They had just a few companions and appeared to be headed to another afternoon of sermonizing.

My face went hot. My stomach swam. I could feel their eyes with the skin of my neck. Goliath was upon me. What else could I do? *If I don't fight, who will?*

In a definitive move designed more to force myself to act than to make any particular dramatic point, I spun around and faced the small party head-on. They stopped and stared. We must have been quite a sight: them in their scholarly regalia, and me in my jeans and In-N-Out Burger T-shirt.

"Excuse me, sirs. I was wondering if I might have a word with you." I don't know why I spoke in English. I also don't know why I sounded like a character from a Rodgers and Hammerstein musical.

The two Islamic men looked at each other for just a moment and then turned and answered me in flawless English. "How can we help you?"

I could not have predicted this encounter. I had had no time to prepare my remarks. I was on the battlefield, slingshot in hand, but I had forgotten to gather any stones. So I said, "I heard you speaking to the students yesterday."

"Yes," the older of the two said, "I remember you being there. Thank you for spending so much time listening to us. Tell me, what is a young American man like you doing in Albania?"

(How does everybody always know that I am an American?)

"Well, if you must know, I [pause for effect] am a Christian missionary." *There. That should do it,* I thought. *This will heat the conversation up.* "I am here because I serve Jesus."

"That is wonderful," the elder scholar said. He managed to say it with no discernible irony or condescension. "We serve Jesus as well. He is the most inspiring and honorable prophet." Then he explained his devotion to Jesus.

Again their response was a bit of a sermon, going on and on for a few minutes, but I must tell you, I was moved by their unmistakable reverence for the historical Jesus. They spoke of Jesus like he is a real person. They quoted his teachings from memory. They were verbose in their devotion. As I listened, I found myself wishing that more Christians could speak of Jesus as these Muslims spoke.

"How has your time in Albania been?" the younger scholar asked. "How have you passed the time?"

"Our work is going quite well. Our time here has been very successful." Then, out of habit I returned the question. "How is your work going?" I couldn't believe that I asked it. Instead of throwing stones, I was lobbing softballs.

"I would say that we do no work at all," he said. "It is God who is at work all around us. It is also not about success or no success. God does not need me for his plans. He also does not need you, young missionary. God is all strength. He does not need you to do his fighting for him." Then he clarified. "Be assured, this does not mean that you are not important. It is the opposite. He is inviting you to sit and watch him perform his wonders. Sometimes he will even let you take the credit. That is what humility does."

Our conversation only lasted maybe twenty minutes. To my disappointment and relief, there was no battle. There were no harsh words. These two men were humble, kind, compassionate, and encouraging. They even blessed me in all my endeavors.

Later, I thought more about those Muslim scholars in their woolen hats, beards, and long robes. I realized that they looked like the Magi (wise men) in my childhood Nativity set. Who were the Magi, anyway? They were spiritual scholars from the East who honored Jesus. They were not Jewish; at least they didn't appear to be. They were certainly not Christians; there was no such thing as a Christian at that time. Did the Magi hold to all the theological intricacies that we Christians believe today? I somehow doubt that they did. And yet Jesus shares my Christmas crèche with them.

As I walked away from the Islamic scholars, I thought about their precious gifts of words and encouragement. I thought about how they reminded me of God's work in the world and my place in His work. I found myself wishing I knew of God as well as they did.

———

A few days later, Sunday morning came. I put on my only pair of slacks and a button-down shirt and went to church.

I sat in the back row.

I didn't much feel like singing the opening songs. My mind was lost in other things. The events of the week had been hard to absorb. At this moment, most of my thoughts were about my pastor. He had scared me, and I was not sure what to do.

The music stopped, and the musicians took their seats.

Then he got up to preach.

My pastor spoke from the gospel of John. It took him about ten minutes to warm up, and then like so many Sundays before . . . the magic happened. He spoke of Jesus' great love for people and his passion to heal. He spoke of miracles. He spoke about signs. He spoke about love. My pastor was inspiring, honest, and sincere. His affection and reverence for Jesus were undeniable. As I listened, I remembered why I had grown to love and respect him so.

But what am I to do with all his crazy Bible talk? I thought to myself. What was I to do with his creepy book with the blood-red demon on the cover? *What am I to do?!*

The answer welled up from a place deep inside me. It was suddenly perfectly clear: *do nothing, that's what.*

Even though we disagreed on something as foundational as our view of the Bible, that reality did not erase all the other ways that he was a loving and profound pastor to me.

I sat back in my chair with a new peace. I stretched my legs out under the folding chair in front of me. My hands were folded across my tummy. I had an odd little smile on my faith as I accepted my pastor for who he is: complicated, paradoxical, and beautiful. The only issue moving forward was whether or not I am willing to see my pastor as he saw himself, as a "dead rock" reflecting the light of God.

In my newfound peace, my thoughts drifted. I started to think about those regal Islamic evangelists. There were so many ways that they saw the world differently than I, essential and profound ways. The question that washed over me was, am I willing to give them the same paradoxical respect as I could give my pastor . . . or the moon, for that matter?

Could I simply accept them for who they are? Could I honestly consider their spiritual insights, even though they were not Christians like me? Could I even allow them to teach me? Could I allow them to be gift-giving characters in the Nativity play of my life?

7

———

SANCTUARY

OCCASIONALLY I WOULD GET A CHANCE TO TRAVEL TO AN Albanian village. I am not talking about an outlying city, or even a small town. These were mountainside villages, consisting of only a few hovels. There are hundreds of such communities across Albania's vast and dangerous ranges. Some of them were located in places entirely unexpected, like a tight valley between two peaks, with terraced fields above and below.

To get to these isolated communities, we would travel by Land Rover, at least as far as the wheels could take us, and then walk in along donkey trails.

When we arrived, we would ask for an elder or civic leader. Often children would be sent, bounding up over footpaths, a simple but effective means of communication. It is odd even now to think that I was most probably the first foreigner to walk along those trails and enter those lovely, humble homes.

We would soon find ourselves sitting in a small living space, next to a freshly stoked fire. These highlanders were simple folk but full of honor. Within minutes I had a warm cup of mountain tea in my cold hands. Our business rarely lasted more than a day, and though we were strangers, we were always offered a warm bed. I was treated like a long-lost relative.

Dinner was always, *always* the best they had to offer. Each time I insisted that they not make a fuss, but there was no discussion to be had. It was easy to imagine that a month's resources were spent on a single meal.

My definition of hospitality will never be the same.

True hospitality pushes past what we can afford to give up and makes deposits in accounts we can never lose.

———

In the summers, when the university was not in session, I would moonlight in the Albanian frontier, working as a project coordinator for various religious agencies. Hundreds of expatriates would come for summer projects. We would coordinate dozens of Albanian students to serve as guides, translators, and coworkers.

We worked from rudimentary but efficient base camps on the edge of the mountainous frontier. One summer, our camp was in an abandoned warehouse. Another, it was in a crumbling castle (a personal favorite). The weeks were long, and there was rarely a day off, but the work was fulfilling, and it was certainly never boring.

I was an odd choice to have so much responsibility, just a clumsy kid still in his early twenties. My duties included training, coordinating teams, organizing transportation, gathering supplies, and communication. I will not bore you with the details, but there was one aspect of my job that I want to share with you now.

———

It was a late July evening. The VHF radio sprang to life just after eleven o'clock at night. Our last radio check-in had been hours before, and the next was not scheduled until seven in the morning. On this particular night we had fifteen teams in the field. I was about to find out that one of those teams was in real trouble.

The voice on the other end of the CB-style radio was desperate. Bill, the old radio operator, yelled up the stairs to me from the radio room. Half-dressed and pulling a shirt down over my head, I jumped down the crumbling stairway. The tone in Bill's voice was unmistakable.

"The house is surrounded, " the team exclaimed. "We are really scared. I don't think we can last until morning. Over." This was not the first time a late-night call like this had come in, and it certainly would not be the last.

I took the handset from Bill. "Please tell us your exact location and describe your circumstances as best you can. Over."

I leapt over to the wall-mounted map of northern Albania. They gave the name of the village, and by this time it only took a moment for my fingertips to find the miniscule dot in a river valley about ninety minutes away. I traced backward from the village to our location. I thought to myself, *If we take this riverbed through the valley, we should be able to shave off some valuable minutes.*

"Todd!" I yelled. I wouldn't dare take this trip alone.

Bill kept jotting down details that he would relay to us while we were en route. I sprinted out the door with Todd close behind. I whipped the keys to Happy off the hook near the door. (Each of our Land Rovers was named after one of the Seven Dwarfs; Happy was emerald green, and though one of the oldest Rovers, he was my favorite.)

The benzene engine roared to life, and we were off. There was no one else on the roads this time of night. Even the police didn't seem to care how fast we drove. So, we flew. Happy could seat twelve people, and still he could maneuver with the best of them.

Todd was on the radio, taking down details. It was impossible to be prepared for moments such as this, so we needed all the information we could gather.

Twenty minutes out, I tore off the highway and down into the riverbed. It was midsummer, the hottest time of year, and the low water left a wide bed of river rock. The unpredictable terrain was a risk, especially driving at night, but it allowed us to cut straight through the valley, saving valuable time. Large rocks and logs were relatively easy to avoid. The real trick is to watch through the bouncing headlights for any long, narrow patch of shadow. A surprise ravine would end us. More than once Happy's wheels left the ground.

We covered the distance in just over an hour. The village contained one narrow road, a cart path, really, not fit for a Land Rover. We drove it anyway. Our headlights revealed our destination immediately. The crowd of two dozen villagers turned to face us. They were startled by our sudden arrival and our growling engine. Their surprise, however, did not mask their anger.

Here's what I could see. Through the small home's side window, I saw fear-filled eyes. Outside the house I saw a small crowd, agitated, filling the path and spilling around the sides of the home. Between the crowd and the house stood a man and his son, maybe fourteen years old. The man had one hand on his son's shoulder, and the other he held up, letting everyone know that by his honor, he would never allow any of them to enter.

It was a standoff.

I left the engine running and jumped out onto the path. Todd and I had been through this before. We had a routine that had worked previously, and we prayed it would work again. We exchanged no words. It was time for action.

I went to the far side of the crowd, away from the house. With as much charm as I could muster, I pleaded to speak to whoever was in charge. While I distracted the crowd, Todd slipped into the house to check on the family and team.

Utilizing every ounce of my imperfect language skills, I kept the crowd distracted. "You—you, sir—you must be the man in charge. I can see that you are a person of great power. Tell me what is going on here."

In response, several voices piped up, explaining the justice of their actions. The shouts came from different places in the crowd.

"We are a Muslim village!"

"We do not want these Christian missionaries here!"

My adrenaline was surging. They were angry for sure, but there was also fear in their eyes. I had heard many tales of old, superstitious religious leaders who would warn villagers against missionaries, threatening the loss of heaven to anyone who helped or even listened to any foreign Christian. How could I possibly compete with the threat of eternal damnation?

I could not concern myself with that now. I had only one responsibility: evacuate our team. And so, I was going to use every negotiation tactic at my disposal to get us out safely. "I understand that you are Muslims, and Muslims are honorable people. But I never thought I would see the day that honorable Albanian people would not show hospitality to the visitor. These people came to your village in peace, and you have given them only fear."

I went on like this for a while, bantering back and forth about the honor of Albanian culture, complimenting the villagers one moment and then shaming them the next, anything to keep them talking. While I spoke, I kept backing up, one step at a time, taking the crowd farther and farther away from the home. All the while Todd worked to get our team out of the house and into the back of the Rover.

Once everyone was in the Rover and Todd was behind the wheel, I played my final card.

With all the authority I could summon, I declared, "It is very late. We must go and leave this honorable village. There will be no more trouble in your village. Thank you. Good night. God bless you." It was the moment of truth. I turned and marched past the crowd without looking back. Todd had two hands clamped around the steering wheel and his foot held above the accelerator.

As I climbed into the passenger's seat, I looked out. Time stopped. I saw only the family who had protected this small missionary team. They stood huddled in the front doorway. The man stood resolute with his hand still on his son. His wife was visibly shaking slightly under his arm.

Then Todd spun the Rover around and we were gone, swallowed by the darkness.

———

I have heard about an old custom of the church—a responsibility, really—to provide sanctuary. Any person, no matter who he is or what he had done, was permitted sanctuary within the walls of the church, for protection. I imagine that a church practice such as this was a tremendous risk. Most of the people who needed sanctuary were probably running from civil authority, and more often than not, they were people despised by society: rejected, outcast, alone, fearful. The church chose providing refuge over maintaining public support. It sacrificed its own safety and security for the outsider. The people of Jesus felt it a sacred duty to provide shelter and protection for the accused and hated.

———

On the ninety-minute ride home, none of us spoke. Happy rumbled along. Our five frightened passengers dropped asleep, exhausted. Todd took the long, safe route home. I stared out the window as the moonlit Albanian frontier flashed by.

I was lost in thought. What had that small family sacrificed to protect these strangers who now left them behind? What had this night's events cost them? It had certainly cost them respect. Had it cost them friendships and status? How about their honor? Was that intact?

There was little doubt in my mind that they had faced real danger. They had done it for strangers, people they would never see again. What would compel a man to risk his family? I prayed that there would be no physical repercussions, especially not tonight. I shot my prayers out into the darkness. I prayed the family would go to bed that night safe.

But what would happen in the morning? This Muslim family had protected Christians. In a village of just a few dozen families, what would this mean? *Will this affect their future safety? How will it impact their livelihood?* Were their small crops or few belongings at risk? How could I know? All I knew is that this evening had been truly frightening.

Then I thought about the man and his son. What had that village boy learned standing next to his father that night? He witnessed character. He witnessed the best example of strength. He learned about virtue and honor. He learned what it really means to care for the weak and unprotected.

Whatever that boy had been taught by his father that night, I wanted the man to know that he had been my teacher as well. I wanted to tell him that I would never forget him.

True hospitality pushes past what we can afford to give up and makes deposits in accounts we can never lose.

8

REVELATIONS

I WAS RAISED TO BELIEVE IN A TWO-TEAM WORLD CONSISTING OF the spiritual haves and have-nots. Christians are the "haves." Everyone else are the "have-nots."

I can't believe in that world any longer. I don't know how many teams there are out there. Some days I wonder if God is the only team. He is the one who is creatively communicating to all of us from an eternally diverse palette.

That seems to be the way it was with Jesus. He did not always teach by pointing to Temple or Torah. Sometimes his text was as unexpected as, "Look at the flower . . . Consider the bird." He even had the courage to point to a pagan and say, "Nowhere in Israel have I found such great faith."

This begs the question: Was Jesus supporting some form of mushy universalism, where everyone is the same—Kumbaya? I would say no. In fact, it is not a commentary on people at all (or birds or flowers, for that matter). Jesus was instead making a comment on his Father, his heavenly Father, his Father who is free. He was declaring that the Father is an unhindered communicator.

I, on the other hand, am the one who is stuck. Not God. I am the one who walks through the world, dividing its elements up into two baskets. In one basket there are elements that I give permission to be conduits of God's voice to me: the Bible, Christians, and anything that one might be allowed to sell in a religious bookstore. In the other basket are those things that God could not possibly be able to speak to or through . . . like a Muslim.

Slowly, and with much kicking and screaming by me, God showed me that the place of hindrance was not in the religious validity of the other person; the hindrance was instead in me. I am the one who is limited. I am the one who struggles to hear. Do I have the spiritual ears to hear God, wherever he might speak? Do I have the spiritual eyes to see God, wherever he might be?

Throughout this season of my life, this revelation of God's courage and creativity was most often pressed upon me by my life with Muslim people.

Before I close this section, here are three final illustrations of ways the truth of God's way was opened to me through life with Muslims.

IMAGE

My dad was raised on a central Oregon ranch. I am the descendent of American pioneers. When the early citizens of the United States spoke about the end of the American story, the trail ended in Oregon.

My father is a good man. Before he died he was known by everyone as a man of character, virtue, and the sort of wisdom that comes from a life well lived and connected to the land. He was also fiercely independent. I rarely saw him ask for help. I never heard him admit weakness. He determined and created his own life.

There are only a few times when I heard my father speak words of delight toward me. That was his way. He did not speak much, and when he did, his words were rarely the musings of the heart. The few times that his delight for me leaked out, it was to affirm my independence.

He loved to see me not need him.

He loved to see me not need anyone.

One of his proudest moments was the day I climbed on a plane for Albania all alone. It is strange to think that I traveled to the other side of the world to feel close to him.

━━━━━

I quickly loved my Albanian family. I loved them all. And they were effusive toward me.

However, one point of frustration for me was my Albanian "uncle" Ari. Ari was the grown brother of Ani, and Fidnet's other son.

Ari was strong, handsome, and smart. When I met him, he was probably in his late twenties. He lived at home with his family. He had almost no space of his own and from my observation, very little life of his own. How could a man so smart and able be satisfied being stuck with his family? I, on the other hand, had left home at age seventeen and had hardly looked back.

I tried to convince myself that I was annoyed by Ari's lack of ambition. However, the more I examined my heart (and the wounds of my independence), the more I discovered that I was actually bothered that he could be content living so integrated with others. The idea that he lacked ambition was a lie anyway. It was something that I had made up to justify the dissonance inside me. It was a convenient accusation since my sense of independence was the only thing I had to be proud of.

Living in Albania, I started to notice other differences from the way I had been raised.

Every day, I would meet new people. I got a chance to hear

their stories. I began to notice that Albanians spoke of their lives in subtle ways that showed a different sense of self, a different view of identity.

Albanians tended to begin their stories with communal terms, not individual ones. Let me try to explain. Most of the people I grew up around used terms of individual identity and personal production to define themselves: *I am a lawyer. I am an athlete. I am an engineering student. I am a pastor.* Albanians, on the other hand, would begin by placing themselves within a communal context: family, village, faith, nation.

It is not that Americans do not use those communal categories as well (or Albanians, individual categories); the difference is where each places the priority. Which one comes first? Where is the greatest value held?

At first this was just a smarty-pants observation of cultural differences. It was not a matter of good or bad, just a matter of distinction. (At least that is what I told myself, though I was also happy to point out the superiority of American pragmatism, production, and innovation.)

However, in time, these communal categories began to seep into my consciousness. It began to affect the way I saw myself. It began to affect the way I saw my faith.

I started to notice that the people of the Bible seemed to see themselves more as Albanians do. There was a great emphasis on family, nation, and tribe. There seemed to be an identity connection to heritage. Bible people saw themselves in the story of their grandparents' grandparents. I, on the other hand, felt I needed to write a fresh story. (In truth, I never thought about my grandparents' grandparents.) I began to understand why my Bible wasted its time (and mine) with long genealogies and books like Numbers.

Then one day I saw something that changed my life. It was

almost twenty years ago, and my life has not been the same since, and those darn Albanians are at least partially responsible for it. I was starting the process of reading my Bible through from beginning to end, when I came upon these words on my Bible's first page: "Then God said, 'Let *us* make mankind in *our* image.'"

God's self-declared identity is communal. Could it be that our identity is communal as well?

ALMS

I never got a chance to be around poverty growing up. We lived in nice neighborhoods in nice parts of town. It was all quite nice. Even when we climbed inside our nice cars to drive crosstown to the nice shopping mall, we never had to see the poor. We had nice roads that would take our car up and over poor neighborhoods or far around them.

Suffice it to say, then, that life in Albania was a shock to the system in the realm of poverty. Beggars were everywhere. And I was an obvious mark. Decrepit old women and filthy children filled intersections and bridges, hands always out, mumbling some excuse to induce you to give them your money. They would tug on my clothes. Sometimes they would sneak up behind me and grab my hand. I could feel the crusted dirt and the open sores.

I had been well educated in the psychology of the beggar, or so I thought. I had been taught that one had to be very careful not to enable that culture. You could never be sure what they were going to use the money for. Were they thieves? Were they addicts? I had even learned that there were intricate criminal networks that stole children and forced them to beg in the streets. The most gruesome stories were of children who had been burned, broken, blinded, or rendered misshapen to increase their ability to garner sympathy. I was a person of virtue; I knew that I did not want to encourage that sort of criminal abuse. Out of virtue, I would keep my money in my pocket, where it would be safe.

One day, I was walking through town with my friend Beni. We were talking away about life and school. As we crossed a bridge, he pulled a handful of bills from his pocket. As we passed beggars, he would meet each one with a look into the person's eyes. "Here you go, beautiful woman." "Here you go, lovely child." He made no show of it; it was just a simple act of kindness. I knew that Beni had very little money, and yet here he was, giving it away.

"Aren't you worried about what they will do with your money?" I asked.

"No."

"I know enough about beggars to know that we should be very careful when we give, and about who we give to."

"Tony, you have so much, and they have nothing."

I almost blurted, "I don't have that much," but quickly stopped myself. I thought for a moment and then responded, "That is not the point. I want to give. Only, when I give, I want to know that I am being truly helpful." I thought that sounded thoughtful and still genuinely concerned.

"Maybe your giving is for you and not for them."

I stopped walking and stared at Beni. I tried to understand what he was attempting to communicate.

He tried to explain. "Maybe it is for your soul. When you look at them, maybe you are looking into the face of God."

I told him, "That is not how faith works!" And I left it at that. Soon after, I read these words:

I tell you the truth, whatever you did for one of the least of these brothers of mine, you did for me . . . For I was hungry and you gave me something to eat, I was thirsty and you gave me something to drink, I was a stranger and you invited me in,

I needed clothes and you clothed me, I was sick and you looked
after me . . .

—Jesus

PARADLE

I was taught that the Old Testament was essentially a long introduction to the New Testament and that the Gospels were mostly
just children's stories. Therefore, I believed that the letters of the
New Testament were the real Bible.

The emphasis of my religious education was on the memoriza-
tion of facts. It was like I was being trained to be on a Bible quiz
team . . . Wait a minute. I really *was* on a Bible quiz team . . .

So, I came to Albania armed with facts about religion. I soon
discovered that Albanians often talked in stories. I had a problem.

What we have here is a failure to communicate.

As a matter of survival, I learned to tell stories as well. For
several months I only had a handful of verbs and a very small vocabulary. (As I said before, language learning has never been a strength
of mine.)

Every day I would sit over meals with my Albanian family. There
was never, ever silence. Someone was always talking, and usually the
speaker was telling a story. I learned to fully participate, substituting
hand motions for verbs and facial expressions for descriptors.

In time, over a thousand conversations about faith with Muslim
people, I learned an unexpected idea. When I stated a fact about
faith, it led to a spirited debate. The argument was often enjoyable,
but there was an undeniable sense that the relational separation
was growing. However, when I shared a story about how I came to
believe what I believe, the relational distance closed like the bellows
on an accordion.

My unexpected discovery was this: facts are the language of
the head; story is the language of the heart. The language of the

73

head encourages debate. The language of the heart encourages friendship.

Years later I was reading Eugene Peterson's translation of the New Testament, and I found these words:

> All Jesus did that day was tell stories—a long storytelling afternoon. His storytelling fulfilled the prophecy:
>
> > *I will open my mouth and tell stories,*
> > *I will bring out into the open*
> > *things hidden since the world's first day.*

No wonder people loved to spend the day listening to him.

ALONE AND AWAY

9

CATHEDRAL

HAVE YOU EVER LOST SOMETHING INTIMATELY PRECIOUS? HAVE you ever lost your hopes or a significant dream? Have you ever, because of your own pathologies, squandered away your reputation or sacrificed your honor? Have you ever experienced rejection from your closest friends or the loss of your life's love?

Have you ever experienced all these things in just under a week?

I did.

After leaving Albania, I had one humble goal: to change the world.

I did not know how I would do it. But I was obsessed with the thought that for my life to truly have meaning, I needed to leave an indelible mark on the world by the time I was thirty. Writing these words now, in my early forties, I realize that I sound insane.

Then again, I think I was insane.

Someone asked me once to describe what "faith" is like for me. It was an odd question, to be sure. I had been asked many times *if* I believed or *what* I believed. I had been asked to choose between two opposing positions, but I had never been asked to describe my experience of "faith."

After thinking for a few minutes, I said something like this. "When I listen to many people talk about their faith, in particular their Christian faith, it seems like their sensation of faith is like a charming couple, in the 1930s, out for a Sunday afternoon drive in the country. The top is down and the air is warm. She has a parasol, and he wears a smart bow tie. Perhaps they are singing as they drive. Occasionally the man playfully swerves the car back and forth across the empty road. She in turn giggles and says, "You are such a rogue."

I am jealous of these people. I am jealous of their faith.

For me, faith doesn't feel anything like a Sunday drive in the country. Mine feels more like a car driving seventy miles per hour on a windy cliff-top gravel road. I am the driver, and I accelerate out of every steep curve just to see: Will the wheels hold the corner or will they simply slip over the edge?

In the years following Albania, the wheels of my faith became worn and frayed. My last stretch of cliff-top road took me into the former Yugoslavia. It proved to be the most difficult stretch of my life yet, and despite its difficulty, I changed nothing about my driving habits.

As you might suspect, one day my faith-tires no longer held the corner.

My soul tumbled off the road, and I died. If you had been there, if you had seen me, you may not have known I was dead: I still walked around; I talked to people; I even worked particularly long hours, but I was dead all the same.

After a while the dead start to stink.

In the end, I was, quite reasonably, rejected by my coworkers and shamed by my leadership. I was moved to Budapest, Hungary. Apparently, Budapest is a holding tank for missionaries with dead souls. I did not know that.

I was there for six months. It was the darkest and loneliest six months of my life.

The funny thing is that only then, saturated in my failure and loneliness, did I finally realize I was dead.

Now I had another, more daunting problem to solve: How do I wake back up?

Those Budapest days were spent mostly by myself. Those months are more or less just a blur to me now. I would wander the streets and slip mindlessly in and out of shops. Some afternoons I would climb on the circle tram. I would ride for hours, staring out at the passing architecture, my cheek resting against the thick, cold window. The nice thing about a circle tram is that you never need to get off. It runs in a circle. It was quite literally a train going nowhere. And I was its most ironic passenger.

In an attempt to jar myself awake, I would go to church. I was taught that there were certain places that were good for the soul and many more that were destructive to the soul. Budapest had plenty from the latter category; church was most definitely at the top of the former.

So, I attended the local international church. You can find these multinational congregations in most major cities of the world. This one had the structure and rhythm of any church my family would have attended back home. My programming insisted that this was the right place to enliven my soul. Church is certainly the place you go to find new life.

I tried to connect. I really tried. I sat in the pew and thought, *Soul, wake up!*

It was no use. The music was just noise. The sermon was just noise. All I could hear was static in my head. It trumped everything. When the service ended, I walked back and forth through the crowd, but it was no use. We were like characters in a science-fiction movie where one guy is moving in slow motion and everyone else is moving at normal speed. The normal people can't even see the slow-motion guy.

———

A few days later, I was riding the circle tram again. My head was resting again against the glass. I wasn't sleepy. Only my soul was tired. My eyes were closed, but I don't know for how long. In time, they half opened. Through the thin slits, cars, buses, shops, and buildings went by. Then, half a block up a passing boulevard, I saw an ancient church with tall spires, like something from a Hugo novel.

I grabbed my bag, slung it over my head and shoulder, and took my place at the stair in front of the exit doors. A bell dinged and the tram stopped. I climbed down and retraced the tracks back to find the church.

Within a few minutes I was standing at the base of the stairs before the wide ornate facade. I had to drop my head all the way back against my shoulder blades to see the tall gable and spires penetrating the cloudy blue.

I trudged up the stairs and tried the door. It was open, and I slipped into the darkness. The inside was cavernous. The ceiling rested several stories above my head. The details were intricate. I read once that old churches were built to emulate heaven. I needed heaven.

I walked down the center aisle and took a seat in one of the worn wooden pews at the center of the sanctuary. At the front of the great expanse hung Jesus. He was alone, just like me.

I closed my eyes. My prayer yelled out within me, *Wake me up! Please, wake me up!*

I listened.
No response.
I tried again. *Wake me up!*
All I heard was the static. I waited for over an hour. It was no use. Inside me dwelled death and static, nothing else.

———

The weeks crawl by when you are bereaved, broken, and bored. I would spend whole afternoons sitting in a teahouse or staring at a cinema screen, anything to pass the time.

A couple of years before, a friend had introduced me to the Hungarian bathhouse. There were a dozen or so of them around the city, an inheritance from the Ottoman Empire. They were a natural application of the mineral-rich water of the Danube basin. Since the fall of Communism, most of these beloved national landmarks had become playful destinations for tourists and coeds. The one I knew about was among the last holdouts of the old way. It was called the Rudas (pronounced "Rood-azh"). It was sunk into the rock at the base of a cliff, on the edge of the river.

The heavy glass front doors and the elongated lobby reminded me of the waiting room in any small European train station: long, formed wood benches, green tiled floor, and an arched ceiling. I crossed the room quickly and took my place in line at the ticket counter. When my turn came, I stepped to the window. I tried to smile at the grumpy woman behind the glass. She didn't care. Without waiting for me to speak, she held up some Hungarian currency, indicating the cost of entrance. I fished out of my pocket the equivalent amount. She handed me a narrow piece of cloth the texture of cheap hotel sheets and pointed me to the locker room.

I took my cues from the middle-aged men around me. I removed all my clothes and hung them in a locker. Then, watching the others, I fastened the tiny cloth around my waist. It did not cover much.

Following the others, I found myself in a dry sauna with tiled walls. I crept back into the steamy cave. There were three consecutive rooms, each with benches for no more than fifteen. Each room was hotter than the last. I climbed all the way to the back and sank into the darkness.

When my naive skin could handle no more, I wandered into the main bathing room. For a boy from Oregon, no place could have been more foreign. It smelled of sulfur and eucalyptus. There was a large octagonal central pool encircled by eight pillars, upon which rested eight heavy arches. I felt I had walked into an Indiana Jones movie. Outside the pillared circle sat four more pools. Above each pool hung a tiled sign indicating the temperature in degrees Celsius. They ranged from arctic to tropical.

Wide-eyed, I stepped deeper into the room, stopping beneath one of the thick stone arches. Above the central pool was a cascading dome. Cut into the domed rock were several dozen circular holes the size of dinner plates. Each hole contained colored glass, like celluloid spotlights in a playhouse. Sunlight streamed through, borrowing the celluloid colors and painting pillars of light through the thick, hanging steam.

Doughy Hungarian men sat half immersed in the various pools. Most of them had discarded their loincloths, using them instead as balled-up sponges to squeeze water over their backs and faces. I imagined them to be Hungarian mafioso. They were the kings, and this was their kingdom. I pitied the person who dared to desecrate their private domain.

The coldest pool was almost empty. I went to it first. I slowly but deliberately dipped down into the water. I let its icy fingers climb inside my pores and shock my senses.

When I could stand it no longer, I climbed out and trotted to the warmest pool. The rich, warm minerals poured into the now-exposed pores.

I had no idea what I was doing. To be honest, I was just thankful to feel something. I took several shifts, switching back and forth between hot and cold until my muscles cried, "Uncle" and my skeleton surrendered.

Finally, I determined to brave the center pool. I stepped all the way inside the pillared circle for the first time and stood with my toes hanging over the green, illumined water. Stairs descended from each of its eight sides like a wide-tiered bowl. At the center, the pool looked no more than a meter or so in depth. To my left, one carved fountain provided an ever-flowing supply of fresh water from a secret mineral spring. The rhythmic splash of the fountain's flow was the only sound.

My goal was to avoid drawing any attention. I slipped down and sat on the third step, deep enough that just my shoulders and head remained above the water. The pool was the same temperature as my body. I leaned back, resting against the stone stairs. Gravity pulled my head against the top step. My ears were under water, but my face remained just above the surface. The water gently lapped against my cheek. I stared up into the sun-pillared, steamy dome and let my arms and legs extend out and up into the buoyant water.

Then it happened: the most unexpected payoff in the most unexpected place. The static silenced. At first I wanted to dismiss it as impossible. I thought that the rumbling in my submerged ears had drowned it out, but no, that was not it.

The static was actually gone.

For the first time, in too long to remember, my soul rested. My gaze fixed on nothing in particular. I was truly content in my water womb, adrift in the steamy darkness. I released up into the dome a two-word prayer: "Thank you."

———

I became a regular at the Rudas. I would visit a couple of times a week, sometimes three.

I had been raised to be suspicious of bathhouses. Though I had never seen one growing up, I was led to believe that they were places of debauchery; maybe many of them are. All the same, it was strange for me to discover that a bathhouse had become my sanctuary. It was the one place where my damaged soul could rest and maybe even begin the long road back to life.

A few weeks later I lay in that same octagonal pool. My head rested on the same step, my limbs limp and floating again. I stared up through the small celluloid windows that crowded the dome above me. I strained to see through the round openings to the cliff top that hung high above the bath's roof.

Who could have predicted when I drove the car of my faith off that cliff so many months before that my freefall would ultimately come to rest in the pool of a Turkish bath?

10

POPE

THERE ARE FEW GIFTS IN LIFE AS PRECIOUS AS A SPIRITUAL HEALER. I have been raised to believe this. Of course, no one in my church growing up ever used the term "healer." Leaders were referred to as *pastors*, *elders*, or *disciplers* (one who cares for disciples), but they were healers all the same. I have encountered these healers time and again since I was young.

In the tenth grade I was ridiculed in front of my classmates by one of my hippie teachers. There were two kinds of hippies in my town. There were the hippies who were all about peace and love. She was the other kind. Ironically, when we asked her how we should address her, she told us to call her "Beautiful." One week, she had been mocking Christians in class. I raised my hand. I told her that I was one of the people she was talking about. She laughed at me. Then she made me the subject of her ridicule the rest of the week. After several days of this, I went to see my youth pastor. I told him what had happened. He sat and listened to my story. He assured me that I had done nothing wrong. He told me that I had acted like a man, not a boy. He told me that God was proud of me. He told me that he was proud of me. He was a spiritual healer.

While living overseas, I had a mentor named Kathryn. More than once, when I was slumped in failure, she sat with me and walked me through the steps of healing. Once, at a particularly helpless point, she looked at me and said, "I made a decision about ten years ago. I vowed that I would never again follow a pastor who had not known failure. Failure is essential in forming great people. Tony, God is making you into a great person." She was a spiritual healer.

Spiritual healing is a noble calling. I am sure you would agree.

————

The day finally came. After months of waiting, I was escorted out of Eastern Europe. The ballots had been counted. The verdict was in. It is strange for someone like me to have no vote in my own future. That is, however, how submission sometimes works. I was released from the Budapest holding tank. It was determined that my path to religious recovery lay back in Oregon.

The proposed place of healing was a lovely, lawn-encompassed campus on the east side of Portland. Seminary was my hospital, and a steady drip of theology was my treatment.

So I settled in Portland.

I was broke. Most of my small income went to tuition. I shared a tiny Portland apartment with a sublime soul named Stacy. He was quiet and relationally undemanding. Added bonus: he was almost as spiritually adrift as me.

Our apartment could not have been more appropriate for two such as us. It was a couple hundred square feet of dank tunnel under an east Portland home. There was only enough room for a couple of desks, a love seat, and a hot plate. I slept tucked up on the house's foundation. If you can imagine this: a four-foot-high slab of concrete jutted out from the wall and was just wide enough to hold a narrow mattress. I had to step on my desk to climb into bed. I then had to roll under the sheets because there was not enough clearance to sit up. Considering our spiritual poverty, it was the perfect home. Like deadbeat uncles or rodents, we were holed away.

Seminary was a difficult hospital for me. It was not difficult because of the content. It was the sort of content that you might imagine: theology, Bible, New Testament Greek. They were the sorts of topics that one might think could help a guy trying to rediscover faith. However, as the months went on, I found myself doubting that faith would ever be found in a PowerPoint presentation or a research paper.

My numbness slowly started to subside, and like a teenager dropped off at a foster home, I felt anger and despair. *I don't need fill-in-the-blank answers!* I wanted to scream. *I have questions. I need to know that having questions is okay. I need to know that doubt is okay. I need messy conversations, the sort that you can slip around on, like guts on a slaughterhouse floor. I need the freedom to be wrong*, I screamed silently to my classmates and my professors. I needed to be free to cry and to yell.

There was just no space for someone like me . . . someone so out of control.

One of my professors admonished me that the problem was with my will. I just needed to *choose* to believe. I thought long about what he said. I was pretty sure the problem was not with my will; I was pretty sure it was my broken heart.

So I would sit at the back of the room and take notes. I would try to learn through my six hours of solitary, with a straitjacket around my tongue.

When the dismissal bell rung, I would slip under the fence and escape to a local pub. It occupied the first floor of the most un-assuming building on a tree-lined southeast Portland street called Belmont. Its only signage, a lazy shingle swaying near the front door. On it were two words: Horse Brass.

NEIGHBORS AND WISE MEN

Through the dark double doors, my eyes adjusted to the dim. Inside there are antique benches and worn, rudimentary tables, like narrow picnic tables, soaked with generations of ale and nicotine. The black lacquered floor covers a space the size of a basketball court but feels much smaller. The room is segregated into smaller spaces by dark pillars and low railings. The walls, ceiling, and bar are cluttered with British kitsch, beer propaganda, dartboards, and Christmas lights. Writing about it, I realize that it sounds just awful. But you will have to take my word for it: it works.

In time I became one of the regulars. The tortured theology student found a welcome seat down in the pit alongside the rest of the crew: Tin Whistle, the Beret, Warrior Princess, Stalin's Beard, the Hugger, Stump, Gilligan, Acorn, Video-Poker, Tipsy-by-Three, Turtleneck, Moby-Dick, and Ed.

Another of the regulars was named Pope. That is not a nickname. That is his real name. He was long and lanky, several inches taller than me. He walked with a broad, swaying gait. I imagined that he could easily have been the guy striding through the woods in those grainy Sasquatch film clips. With his thick beard and heavy boots, he certainly played the part. Through his thick whiskers, he rarely withheld his toothy grin. His giggle was his greatest gift.

I guessed that he and I were about the same age, though I never asked him. His yellow teeth and skin betrayed a lifetime of hard choices, choices that would take his life a few years later.

———

Pope and I were friends and competitors. We competed at the dartboard and we competed over words. Pope was an argumentative son of a gun. There are few diatribes as dramatic as the ones found in an ale-fueled beer hall. Pope and I had gone twelve rounds more than once over issues of faith, politics, or whether or not one could justify being a fan of the NBA. The difference was, we were free to disagree—and to lose control. And the most caustic arguments would devolve into laughter. In the end we would not invalidate each other. Instead we would buy each other a beer and throw a game of darts.

One afternoon I was sitting at my favorite table under the wide-paneled front window on the pub's north side. I was pecking away at my computer, trying to complete an assignment that was infuriating me more and more by the minute. Pope was sitting at the bar, smoking a cigarette. He must have noticed the agitation in my face and in the clacking from my keyboard. Amused, he came over and straddled the red, vinyl-covered stool across from me.

"Whatcha workin' on?" he asked, most likely overexaggerating his face to feign ignorance and empathy.

"I am trying to finish this paper because I love jumping through hoops," I responded curtly and banged a few more keys. I didn't look up.

Pope, no doubt annoyed that his amusing face had gone unnoticed, crushed out his cigarette in the tray on the table's corner and tried another angle. "So, what did your computer ever do to you?"

"What?!" I shot back and looked up into his furry face. I was met with a grin and playful eyes.

"There you are," he said. "I have been waiting for you. How are you? It's nice to see you. Why don't you take a break and talk to me?" Smile.

I closed the computer screen and let out a long exhale through my closed lips in that way that makes them sound like a motorboat. "I think I need to quit school."

"Why?"

"I am studying Christian theology . . . which is funny to me. I have questions that I honestly don't even know how to ask. When others in my classes ask questions, they seem to phrase them in a way that shows that they 'get it.' My problem is that I *don't* get it. I don't even think that I believe the same way the others do. I don't care about having the right answers, at least not like they do. I just want to know that what I believe has real meaning, meaning in my heart and in the real world."

Pope watched my glazed-over eyes and said, "Hmm. And you think being a quitter will somehow help you find meaning in the real world?"

I think he intended to be snide when he said it, but because of his heart, it actually came out sincere, probably to his disappointment.

Pope and I bantered back and forth for the better part of an hour. He grilled me about my motivations, whether or not education is a gift and the nature of religion. A couple of times our agitated voices could be heard from the other side of the bar.

Finally Pope said, "Man, on the one hand you have a problem with Christianity. Since I study the Kabbalah, I have no dog in that fight. But I do know that I care about you. And I know you. I know that you want to follow God. So here is what I want to know, and I want you to answer honestly. Do you think God can guide a person?"

"Yes," I answered nervously.

"Do you think God guided you to be my friend?"

"Actually, I do."

"Do you think God wants good things for you?"

"Yessssss," now more nervous.

"Do you think that God is able to care for you and teach you through your classes and professors?"

I just sat in silence. I didn't know what to say.

After a few moments Pope lit another cigarette. He took a long drag and blew the dancing smoke into the air between us. Then, gesturing toward me with the cigarette between his fingers, he said, "I have plenty of regrets in life. More than I can name. I have quit plenty of things, and thus"—he paused for effect—"you have the

man before you today." As he said it, he held his arms wide so I
could get a good look at him. He held the pose for several seconds
and giggled loud enough for the whole bar to hear.

His laughter subsided, and he knocked his ash into the tray.
"Here's the deal, brother . . . You are fighting the wrong fight. There
is nothing wrong with your classes. They are a gift. You are going
to get a graduate degree, for God's sake. Your problem is you think
faith is about the lectures and the assignments. You think your faith
is in your head. Faith is not in your head; it is about the heart." And
he reached his long arm across the table and tapped me on the left
side of my chest. "Let God guide your heart. All right? I don't know
if that is good advice, but that's all I got." Then he crushed out his
cigarette, stood up, and walked away. But he stopped and looked
back with a wink. "Oh, and don't quit."

From that day forward Pope became the cheerleader of my education. He also continued to be a massive pain in my derriere.

Even now, it is hard to describe why the Horse Brass pub provided such a unique place of healing for me. It was odd that I felt
so at home there. Up to that point I had spent very little of my
life inside a bar. My first drink of alcohol was on my twenty-first
birthday, a glass and a half of beer purchased by a belligerent band
of friends.

Maybe it is because the pub doesn't have an agenda. A pub
doesn't have a regimented road. So much of my life was a series of
rutted paths. Whatever the topic, the conversation seemed to settle
into a well-ridden rut. The ruts were approved and predictable. The
ruts were safe.

I didn't need safe. I needed to explore off the path, away from
the ruts. I needed to rip off my shirt and run madly, my arms

flapping, through an untamed field. I needed healing friends who were comfortable with my madness.

In the end it wasn't the pub at all. It was the people: sincere and patient ragamuffins who unwittingly supplied my healing time and time again.

11

FAITH

DESPITE MY DEPRESSION AND SELF-DESTRUCTION, THE TIDE OF MY faith slowly started to roll back in.

It was nice to be able to believe again. It was nice to start, just start, to find healing in the words of my Bible again. It was nice to be able to pray again.

Growing up, one of the big divisive issues among Christians was around the question, "Can you lose your faith?" It was hotly contested in the circles in which I traveled. I came from a tradition that insisted that one could never lose his or her faith: "Once saved, always saved." Spiritual life insurance was an irrevocable contract.

I can remember being a young man and being trained in the art of ministry. My trainer, John, explained to me that when ministering to another person, there was no question as essential as, "If you were to die tonight, on a scale of 1 to 100, how sure are you that you would go to heaven?" Trainer John taught me that I should never abandon a ministry conversation unless this all-important question had been satisfactorily answered with those eternal words: "I am 100 percent sure."

Trainer John insisted, "If they say they are 50 percent sure, or 70, or 90 . . . even if they say 99 percent sure, that is not good enough. Simply remind them of the words of Jesus: 'I will never leave you nor forsake you.' Then ask them again, 'How sure are you? Do we take Jesus at his word or don't we?' Help them see that there is no doubt. Faith must be unwavering. It must be confident to be true."

I wonder what Trainer John would say to me after the roller coaster of my last few years? I went from a triumphant Christian missionary with the sort of spiritual confidence that would have made him proud to a defeated doubter with a dead soul. According to the "once saved, always saved" paradigm, he could not say that I "lost my faith." That is not possible. Would he say that I had simply never been a true Christian and my last couple of years were irrefutable evidence of that fact?

There was no doubt that I had violently wavered. Would he say that my only hope of salvation lay in the future? Therefore, was my past a waste? With sincere love, I am sure he would pray that someday I would discover a true and finally unwavering faith in God.

———

I met Katarina one afternoon at the Horse Brass. She was quite a sight to behold inside the dank British pub.

She glided through the front door—floated, really. To watch her move you would never have guessed she was in her sixties. Unashamedly, she used little makeup and wore her white hair long and free. Her clothes were as colorful as her spirit. She had a long, flowing skirt and a wide silken scarf hung loose over her shoulders and draped over her torso.

Katarina stopped at the base of the stairs in front of the bar.

She stood under the cross-stitched sign declaring "Yanks Welcome" and spun around, perhaps looking for me, but more so taking in the details of the worn and weathered public house. I watched her. She absorbed every element: black and white photos of wartime Britain, antique Guinness posters, and glowing stained glass under dark-wood rafters.

She finally saw me in the far corner booth, sitting under the "Britain Wants You" war poster and a painting of boats at sea, signed by an artist ironically named Fisher.

She floated to the table and said, "This place is wonderful." Her voice was breathy with delight.

Katarina and I had met at a wedding a few days before. I learned that despite her six decades of life, she had returned to school. She was working on a doctorate in religion, focusing in ecumenical spirituality. As for her tradition, she was a liberal-minded Jew. She also had an abiding affection for all honest and loving people of faith. On that wedding reception lawn, with champagne flutes in our hands, we had exchanged only a few thoughts, but she was intrigued. She had insisted that we continue our conversation sometime soon. I was hesitant. She would not take no for an answer.

So here we sat. A bald guy in his early thirties, dressed in dull wool and knitted cap, and a vivacious Jewish academic dressed in all the colors of Monet.

Though I was fighting feelings of depression that day, we were having a truly lovely conversation. The first half hour or so was filled with the stories of life and adventure. We talked about family. She told me about her grown children. I shared about my new infatuation with Aimee and how ironic yet wonderful it was to fall in love with someone I met at a seminary. We exchanged notes about travels and compared maps for destinations of overlap. We bantered about Western Europe and shared memories of Israel, particularly art-gallery hunting in the northern town of Safed.

She leaned back in the wooden booth. She talked with her hands. Her smile was bright. I, on the other hand, was far more reserved but still engrossed. I kept both my hands wrapped around the belly of my pint glass, still full.

Then she paused, allowing her last chuckle to dissipate, like a plume of cigarette smoke. After a moment of silence, she looked at me and asked, "Would you please give me the gift of hearing your story of faith?"

"Well . . ." I took a long drink from my glass. Then I wiped my mouth as I thought. I did not want to give her a canned speech. I wanted to tell my story in light of who she is and in the spirit of our newfound friendship.

I started with my childhood faith and growing up in my Baptist church. I told her about my early doubts in high school, doubts that were strong enough for me to pause my faith practice for about a year and a half.

Then I explained the faith adventure of my university years. It was a time of fresh discovery and inspiring spiritual friendships with the most satisfying sorts of Jesus people.

I took my time. She never spoke. Her eyes were fixed on me even though mine were mostly set on the foamy surface of my beer. I would occasionally look up at her. Each time I did, she appeared to be holding her breath, as if she wanted nothing to interrupt my words. My story had never felt so sacred.

I kept walking through chapter after chapter, and she was most content to follow. Eventually, we arrived in the former Yugoslavia, and my cadence slowed further. I told her about the years of seven-day workweeks and sixteen-hour days. I tried to describe the obsession that drove me. She seemed to understand.

"That's when it happened," I said. I chose my words carefully. "That was when my soul died. I don't know how else to explain it." I did not look up as I spoke. I was making a pattern of water rings with the bottom of my glass on the surface of the rough-hewn table.

I kept talking. "You know, I had always been a really disciplined kid, especially in my religious life. Even back in junior high school I would wake up early to spend time in prayer and Bible study. That discipline never left me . . . so when I was twenty-eight and living with a dead soul, I would still get up at six in the morning to try and have time with God. It was ridiculous, really. I was such an idiot. I didn't even believe in God. And even if God did exist, my heart was too dead to care if he gave a s*#! about me." I immediately felt guilty for talking like that.

Moisture started to pool in the corner of each eye. "You know what I would do at six o'clock every morning?" I couldn't look at her. "Since my Bible didn't make any sense to me anymore, I would just kneel next to my bed. I would kneel there with my hands folded on the comforter, the way a child prays. My head was numb. My heart was numb. And this is what I would do. I would chant. I would chant the same words over and over. It was all my heart could manage. 'God, I choose to believe you exist today. I choose to believe you exist today. I choose to believe you exist today.' How ridiculous is that? I couldn't pray for my friends. I couldn't pray for my teammates. I couldn't pray for our work. I couldn't even pray for myself. I was worthless."

At this point one of the pools of moisture overflowed and trickled down my cheek. I quickly wiped it away. "So anyway . . . that was the time when I lost my faith."

My design of water circles had become quite elaborate. I tried to think of what else I should say. I couldn't think where to go next, so I just sat there staring at the water-circle pattern.

When I finally looked up from the table surface and at Katarina, I was shocked by what I saw. Everything about her had changed. All her pleasantness was gone. Her eyes were hot. She was almost shaking.

"How dare you!" She thrust her finger at me when she said it. "How dare you!" She was desperately trying to maintain her composure, but her anger was overwhelming her.

"Don't you ever, *ever* say that again. How dare you speak that way about your faith. How dare you *shame* your story like that. Shame on you!"

She tried to calm down. Her hands were now on the table in front of her. Her fingers, shaking slightly, were slowly tracing the ruts in the wood. "My people waited in silence for generations to hear from God, to be able to talk to him. Generations! We waited in silence. We screamed at the sky. We waited for God to speak."

She looked up from the tabletop and stared intently into my eyes. "Look at me," she demanded. "Look at me and never forget what I am about to tell you. You did not lose your faith. Do you hear me? You did not . . . lose . . . your . . . faith. Your faith was not gone. Your faith was strong. I know it didn't feel like it, but your faith was true, not only because you waited for God, but more important, because even in the silence God was waiting with you."

Katarina sat back again. She labored to reestablish her normal regal posture. She adjusted her scarf so the knot once again hung off center and the silky billows flowed evenly across her shoulder and front. Once satisfied, she cleared her throat. She leaned over slightly and patted me on the forearm. "You are such a dear, sweet, wonderful young man. God has been so very, very kind to you."

I knew she was talking about more than just my words; she was confronting my religious programming, what I believed about my faith.

———

Since that afternoon with Katarina, I have tried to change my perspective on belief. Unfortunately, wherever that belief-switch is inside me, I can't seem to find it. I can, however, change my language, not just for language's sake but because my language both betrays and shapes my inner life. I have tried to speak of my faith experiences with different words. Though I have had times that were full of doubt, darkness, or a feeling of distance from God, I no longer say that my faith was "lost." It is still hard to explain, but I think sometimes our faith is just silent for a while.

Most days I still feel spiritually weak. I have had so much drifting and failure in my spiritual story. Katarina's words have stuck with me. I imagine they will never leave me. She helped me heal. She helped me heal from my past.

I would be very intrigued to hear Trainer John and Katarina discuss faith. I am sure it would be quite spirited. I am certain they would see things in very different ways.

I also have a feeling that Katarina would feel like her time with Trainer John was a great gift. I would also bet that Trainer John would walk away feeling unexpectedly encouraged by their conversation.

12

PROPHET

I WAS FINALLY STARTING TO GET IT: THE PROCESS OF HEALING WAS ultimately God's process. The conduits of that healing were going to come from places I could not control or predict.

One of the most absurd things Jesus ever said was when he told his followers that it was a good thing that he would die and go away. Sometimes he sounded like Crazy Prophet. How could the world possibly be a better place without the Incarnation? How could anything be better without the most wonderful, insightful, wise, creative, loving, truth-emanating, eternity-revealing, God-proclaiming person who had ever lived? How is that even possible?

Like I said, "Crazy Prophet."

Then Jesus explained his crazy claim. He said that when he was gone, he would send the "one who walks alongside" to guide us through this troubled world. Jesus actually believed this Walk-Alongsider would change everything. The Walk-Alongsider would create and communicate wholeness, reveal truth, and make things right. The Walk-Alongsider, with the character of God himself, would utilize Creator power to finish the story.

There is a centuries-old prayer by an unknown author that pleads with God to

> be in the heart of each to whom I speak;
> in the mouth of each who speaks unto me.

This prayer embraces the confidence of Jesus. It expresses belief in the Walk-Alongsider. These two sacred lines literally beg God's Spirit to speak through the mouth of *anyone* who crosses my path.

However, all things need temperance. Don't they? We must be realistic and not take things too far. After all, "my mama didn't raise a fool." Simple wisdom should show us when someone is beyond the scope of this prayer.

Suspicion is a good thing. Isn't it?

———

My second summer back in the States, I was invited to participate in an urban emersion program for college students. It took place in New York City. The concept was that students would come for a summer. They would experience intense personal mentoring while daily engaging the very real social, justice, and spiritual concerns of some of New York's toughest neighborhoods. I was asked to be one of the mentors.

It was a tremendous opportunity for me. It was also a personal victory, validation that I was back on the road to spiritual recovery. At least, so I thought.

The students spent their days with nonprofits, in shelters, and supporting social programs. As a supervising mentor, I got to tag along.

During my first week in New York, I was introduced to one of the oldest homeless shelters in the five boroughs. It was an old, multistory building in a lower Manhattan neighborhood called the Bowery.

Inside, things were about what I might have suspected. My first experience was in the chapel. Here, the "guests" would get a daily dose of the gospel.

It was midmorning. I slipped in and found a pew near the back of the room. I listened to the passionate shelter director share about the healing message of the Bible. "If you will only give your life to Jesus and follow his words, you will be saved."

I thought it was a good message. I thought about all these poor souls all around me who could use some gospel healing.

While listening, I looked around the room. It was narrow. At the front was a small stage with enough room for a podium and, if needed, a couple of musicians. The attendance that morning was spotty, no more than a dozen souls. One bearded man sat against the right wall. He rocked in his seat with the rhythm of the preacher's voice. Another man sat with his arms wrapped around a stuffed duffel bag, his nose on top of the bag, peering over it at the stage.

Behind me and in the corner sat a monument of a man: large, strong, and black. I estimated he was several inches taller than me and outweighed me by at least a hundred pounds. It is sometimes hard to guess a person's age in a place like this. On one hand his face had a childlike quality, but on the other there was rabid wear on his body and soul. I guessed he was about fifty.

Before long the service was over, and I followed the congregants out of the chapel and into the dining room. I found a man back by the kitchen in a long, white apron, carrying a clipboard. I introduced myself and explained that I was working with the summer mentor program and was available to help. He smiled and impatiently shook my hand. I was told to wash my hands and take a place at the buffet. I was on beans.

Over the next forty minutes, fifty or so guests came through the line. Once the volume slowed, I was relieved and encouraged to grab a plate of my own. So I did.

The small dining room was mostly full. The room made me anxious. I don't know how to act around homelessness. A fissure of insecurity cracked open inside me. I passed several tables that were full and intimidating. I then came to a table with the monument-man from the back of the chapel. He sat alone. His back was to the wall. He leaned over his plate, surrounded by empty chairs.

Here goes. "May I join you?" I asked.

He looked up from his plate. Our eyes met. A warm smile appeared. "I would be honored to have the company. Please pull up a chair." He had a Southern accent. Having been raised on the West Coast, I had always been terrible at placing accents, but his was distinct and melodic.

"My name is Tony."

"I'm Harry. So what brings you to my home? Are you a new guest?"

"A guest? No . . . I mean . . . I am not . . . What I mean is . . . I'm perfectly . . . I . . ." I hung my head. "I am just visiting for the day." Could I have handled that worse? "Harry, I am so sorry."

"Oh, don't concern yourself, young man. My skin is thick and my heart is open. You have nothing to worry about with me. If your life is anything like mine, this place is probably a whole universe away from where you were raised." He gave me a minute to get situated and then asked, "Where were you raised, anyway?"

He was pleasant. In between bites I told him my story, at least some of the highlights. Then I asked him about his. He shared about being raised in the South. He told me about his family and his church growing up. He told me about singing in choir on Sunday morning. Then his story jumped abruptly into the last few years and his unexpected life in the streets. He explained that he had been in the shelter for a few weeks and that he was working the program. "You have to work the program to stay," he said. Then he confided what I already assumed: he was an addict. To hear the tone in his voice, you would think him the worse kind of addict imaginable. I tried not to imagine.

"Do you use?" he asked.

"No, never."

"Good. Keep it that way. Drugs will take everything." When he said *everything*, his voice sank low like a grave. I could tell there was a long, dark story behind it, a story he did not volunteer. I didn't ask.

We finished lunch and put our plates away.

Then I turned to say good-bye and thank him for the conversation, but before I could, he said to me, "Can I show you something?"

"I've got nothing but time," I said, trying to sound cool. I missed. He didn't care.

"Well, all right, then; follow me."

He led me through a narrow back hallway and up a stairwell. As I walked behind him, I was amazed at how he eclipsed the passage. After the climb, we walked through a door and into a small lounge. I looked around: couches, a bookshelf, and a few games.

Harry walked over and sat down at an old piano, worn smooth by time. It sat along the same wall as the door we just walked through. "Do you know what this is?" he asked.

Using my mighty powers of perception, I concluded that "a piano" was not the answer he was reaching for. His broad shoulders made the piano look small. I chose not to guess. "I don't know; what is it?"

"This"—as he spoke, he let his fingers glide back and forth across the keys—"this is Fanny Crosby's piano." He said it reverently, like someone talking about a battlefield or the Constitution.

I knew I should have known the significance. He asked, "Do you know Fanny Crosby?"

I gave him an awkward smile and a shrug.

He laughed to himself. "All right. So tell me, young man, do you sing?"

"A little."

"Well, sing one of Fanny's songs with me."

Then he started to play. There was a flourish in his introduction. His huge hands moved like butterflies across the keys. Then his strength sank deep into the keyboard, and he let a single chord fill the small room and tumble down the stairs.

Then he sang. As he did, he looked over at me to join.

"Blessed assurance, Jesus is mine! O what a foretaste of glory divine!"

His voice rang, pure and lovely. I could hardly bring myself to clutter the space with my voice, but he had asked me to join.

"Heir of salvation, purchase of God, born of his Spirit, washed in his blood. This is my story, this is my song, praising my Savior all the day long . . ."

He sang the words more slowly than we did in my Baptist church growing up. His eyes shut; his head looked up. He shook with vibrato. I believed he was singing for God himself, the words crying from deep love. "Watching and waiting, looking above, filled with his goodness, lost in his love . . ."

When he finished, he let the last chord hang in the air; his head now low over the keys.

He sniffled once and spoke to me without looking up. "You know, Tony, Fanny was broken just like me. As a child, she lost her ability to see. As a man, I lost my sobriety, my dignity . . . well, pretty much everything."

Only then did he turn and face me. "God loved Fanny so much that he gave her an amazing gift. He gave her the ability to write songs, thousands of them. That's what God does; he sings his song out through broken things. Do you believe that?"

"Yes."

"Well, I used to believe it . . . and every day I am getting closer to believing it again."

He rubbed his palms back and forth along the tops of his legs. Then he looked up. "Would you like to hear another song?"

I said, "Yes, please."

"Okay then," and he bowed his fingers once again to the keys.

And so we sang, the whole afternoon through, just Harry and me.

———

I came back again a few days later and a few days after that. Usually we spent lunch together and then lingered for another hour or two. It was really wonderful. Have you ever met someone who is just profound? It seems like everything that person says is without platitude or assumption. That kind of person speaks only from the deep place of experience, drawing from a well of pain. Harry was like Gandhi. Okay, maybe not quite Gandhi, but he was as close as I had come across in a long, long time . . . at least most of the time he was.

There was just one small problem: Harry was crazy.

He wasn't always crazy. Not at all. That first day we spent at the piano, he was as sane as Mother Teresa. But then there were the other times.

Usually it was pretty innocent stuff. He would repeat himself or forget things we had just discussed. Those things could be chalked up to the cheese grater that the drugs had taken to his mind.

But other times, he would go off for minutes at a time about imaginary things. Crazy things. For instance, he believed he was friends with Hollywood personalities. Seriously. Can you imagine someone you respect saying, "So, Anthony Hopkins called me, and we were talking about . . ."? Can you imagine? It was impossible for me to accept.

The conversations would go something like this. We would be discussing something, like having courage to live, and he would say, "It is just like when I was talking to Larry Fishburne. Larry would say, 'You will never know if you can do anything until you deny your fear and throw yourself in.'"

The first time I responded playfully, later with pure condescension, "Do you mean Lawrence Fishburne the *actor*?"

"Yes, *Larry* Fishburne." He said it like it was the most normal thing in the world.

At this I would think to myself (remembering a line from *The Matrix*), *Are you sure he didn't say, "You take the red pill—you stay in Wonderland and I show you how deep the rabbit-hole goes"?*

Our times together went on like this for a few weeks. Our conversations were insightful and encouraging one moment, and crazy talk the next. I did not know if it was schizophrenia or just a cheese-grater mind, but it was challenging my capacity to cope. I can handle profound and I can somewhat handle insane, but not at the same time and not from the same person.

The lapses were similar, involving Larry Fishburne or a pantheon of other actors. I knew there was no way he could actually know all these famous people. I'd think, *Just look at him. He is a homeless addict with a Southern drawl. He has no money. He has no life. If he worked really hard, he might someday rise to mere insignificance.* In my darkest moments I felt ashamed that I had held him so highly.

A few times I tried to confront him, but he always insisted that I was the one who did not understand. He did so with a calm certainty that infuriated me all the more. It is one thing for Harry to be crazy; it is another thing for him to question my grasp of reality. It became more than I could bear.

So I stopped coming. Just like that. I stopped. To make matters worse, the last time I had visited him, we'd argued. As I left, Harry had asked me, "Will you come back tomorrow?"

I'd told him, "I will,"

We'd both known it was a lie.

━━━━

More than a week went by. My guilt got the better of me. I thought, *Just because he is crazy, it doesn't mean that I can't at least be his friend. He doesn't have to be my Gandhi; he can just be my crazy homeless friend.*

I arrived at the shelter a little before lunch. I checked in the chapel, and there was no sign of Harry.

Then I waited for lunch, and I watched the crowd come and go. No Harry.

I searched everywhere and eventually found a staff worker. I reminded him who I was, and when it registered, he greeted me warmly with a firm handshake. "What can I do for you?"

"I am looking for Harry. He wasn't at lunch today. Do you know where he is?"

He reached out and placed his hand on my shoulder. "I am sorry. We don't know where Harry is. He left the program about a week ago. He just slipped out, as often happens. Were you friends?"

I answered, "Not really." I immediately knew I could not betray him like that. "Well, kind of. I mean, yes. Yes, Harry is my friend. Do you know when he will be back?"

"I'm sorry. He will never come back. Once they go back to the streets, 100 percent of the time they never come back. That is just the way it is."

I angrily thought to myself, *Harry's a person, not a statistic.* But who was I to be sanctimonious? I am such a hypocrite.

I said good-bye to the shelter worker, and within seconds I was back on the streets.

I spent the better part of the afternoon wandering back and forth from SoHo to Alphabet City, looking in doorways and up alleys. I knew it was hopeless, but I couldn't stop looking. Round and round in my head went the words *He asked me if I would come back tomorrow. I told him, "I will."*

As I stumbled around without a plan, I replayed our conversations again and again in my mind. It was a ping-pong match in my head: profound talk, crazy talk, profound talk, crazy talk.

I can't believe I called him Gandhi, I thought in disgust.

Disgust is an effective antidote for shame.

In desperation I finally talked to God's Walk-Alongside Spirit. I begged, "Help me. Protect my heart from pain like this. Give me wisdom to know when someone is speaking from you and when he can't."

My mind returned to that ancient prayer:

> *Be in the heart of each to whom I speak;*
> *in the mouth of each who speaks unto me.*

How could this prayer possibly mean *anyone?* Though I wanted to believe it, Harry had taught me that I needed to protect my heart.

———

Some weeks later I was with some friends who said they wanted to watch a movie. Dave said he would run to the video store. "What do you want me to get?" he asked.

"We don't care. Just grab anything and hurry back."

It only took Dave about twenty minutes. While he was gone, we arranged the room for maximum coziness. We placed several colorful pillows on the floor in front of the secondhand furniture, arranged in a semicircle around the small apartment's front room. The walls were filled with original art, mostly painted by friends. A smallish tube television sat in a corner opposite the wide front window and would provide our humble movie screen.

When Dave returned, he announced, "I grabbed the first thing I saw. It is a Charlie Sheen movie." We all flopped down together as only a group of singles can.

Dave shoved the videotape into the briefcase-sized VCR and toggled through the credits, pressing buttons on the black machine (the remote control had been lost long ago).

The film was reasonably entertaining with Charlie; his dad, Martin Sheen; and Lawrence Fishburne.

It was hardly an Academy Award candidate, so I was mostly zoning out as the storyline grew. Then, twenty minutes into the film, to my horror, Harry marched onto the screen. That's right; *my* Harry. And for the next two hours I watched Harry carry on conversation after conversation with Larry Fishburne, along with Charlie and Martin, just some of the characters from his "pantheon of insanity."

———

So it ends up Harry wasn't crazy after all. He was right all along; I was the one who did not understand.

This revelation probably should have filled me with shame for how I treated Harry, and it did, but that was not the strongest feeling. The strongest feeling was delight and humor and joy. It was as if the very thing that the Walk-Alongsider had been trying to communicate to me all along, the thing I had refused to hear, suddenly became crystal clear. I left my friend's apartment with a beautiful sense of stillness and harmony inside me.

The question I eventually found myself asking was this: Was

Harry's sanity even the issue? Does his mental state somehow erase the potential for him to be God's voice to me, if I am available to it? Does it erase the ability of God's Walk-Alongside Spirit to speak through his mouth? Does it erase it any more than his physical appearance, his income level, his skin color, his heritage, his sobriety, or his religious tradition?

The fact of the matter is, if I am really honest, I was looking for a reason to dismiss him. And that is on me. Why did I want to dismiss him? Well, I don't know why exactly. It was probably a whole matrix of prejudices at work within me. His alleged insanity was just my most justifiable excuse. If it hadn't been my judgment on his sanity, it would have been his poverty, his addiction, or—dare I admit?—his skin color. That is my brokenness. I am looking for ways to dismiss most anyone, especially if they are different from me. Over the years I have become quite good at it.

How many spiritual gift-givers have I dismissed because of my prejudice, ignorance, and disdain?

13

HOPE

MY FRIEND AYRIC SAID THIS WEEK, "GOD HAS DONE SO MUCH work on me; I am starting to wonder if he has time for anybody else."

I know exactly what he means.

By the time I was thirty, I had spent my entire adult life, almost a decade, as a professional Christian. When I say *professional Christian*, I simply mean someone who gets paid to have faith.

What is faith, anyway?

Early on, I was told that faith is trust in a series of beliefs: God exists, God is just, God is Creator, God speaks through the Bible, Jesus died on the cross, Jesus rose from the dead, and so on.

Later in life I was taught that that those beliefs were in fact not faith at all; they were just the setting, like the trees in a snowy forest. Faith was not about beliefs; faith was about a person, believing in a person. Specifically, being confident in Jesus. That thought was helpful to me.

But I had another problem. Over the years my faith had been contaminated. There were powerful and subtle contaminants that had mixed in with my beliefs and been tenaciously reinforced. This reinforcement was unintentional and without malice, but it was toxic all the same. It came from Dad, culture, church, and mentors. These contaminants had names like *independence, mercenary mentality, validation through accomplishments, comparison,* and a very strong belief that I was generally not wanted around. These false beliefs made life with God impossible. So impossible that God did the only thing that a loving God could do. He took a baseball bat to my life. He shattered my spiritual kneecaps. He busted my spiritual collarbones. Once I was on the ground, with no fight left in me, he reached inside me as if I were a Halloween pumpkin and scooped me out. Then he declared a do-over. That's the way it works with contaminants sometimes. He scooped out my "good" beliefs and my false beliefs. And he chose to start clean.

So I started from no-belief. Not atheism; atheism is anti-belief, which, ironically, is also a belief. Nope, this was just no-belief.

Over time, God and I started to talk again (remember the Turkish bathhouse?). It was nice to be back on speaking terms. Our first year back on speaking terms, God seemed to be interested in only one topic: fatherhood, specifically his fatherly love toward me. Sometimes I would try to expand the conversation, but he patiently steered me back to Father-love. He framed it as a quiet love, a still love. He would say, "Just sit with me. Don't do anything. Right now, I don't care if you never do anything *for* me again. I just want to be with you and you with me. Come . . . rest your head. Rest your heart. Rest your soul."

And so it went, one belief at a time, carefully and quietly planted inside my scooped-out soul.

I had still *another* problem. So much of my understanding of Christian duty had been framed by violence: There are two teams and only one can win. We must take the mountain, kill the giant, win the battle, defeat the enemy, fight for truth. This language had subtly convinced me that I was just a mercenary for God, nothing else.

I was tired of the violence. I had a hard time seeing Christian service any other way. I started thinking about getting out of the game altogether. I daydreamed about a very quiet faith, a very private faith. Maybe Jesus and I could retire. Get a place down in Florida. Maybe take up fishing. Jesus likes fishing.

———

After my return from New York City, I continued to visit the Horse Brass. I joined a dart team. I smoked a pipe. I became a beer snob.

One midweek afternoon, Dennis was at the bar. I always felt more at home with Dennis behind the bar. He was like a dear uncle, a jovial companion, and an innocent enabler all rolled up in one. He wears his gray hair short, and he has rosy cheeks. I knew that if I ever needed a Santa Claus, he would be my first choice. Dennis wears shorts twelve months of the year, accompanied by obscure beer T-shirts, basketball sneakers, and knee braces. He walks with a sway to hide his chronic pain. His knees and back bear the brunt of decades of jerking beer taps and carrying kegs. The pain shows with every step.

After Dennis had finished his shift and closed out his till, he came over and joined me. I was sitting in one of the raised sections of the bar, near the front door, under the East India Company etched mirror. He had a job-well-done beer in his meaty fist and plopped down across from me without asking permission. We didn't need to ask for permission. Dennis and I were past that.

"How are ya?" he asked with his trademark chuckle. "Oh man, my body is beat." Chuckle again, then a long drink from his pint. "So, brother, tell me: How are things going with your theological studies and your work?"

I love Dennis. We had talked on numerous occasions about life and faith. He seemed to find encouragement that I worked to stay in the church. He had shared with me several times about life growing up in a Lutheran family. He had loved religion as a boy, but those days had long since passed.

Months before, Dennis and I had talked about how he had ended up behind this bar for all these decades. "I think I have just seen too many things that broke my heart. My years in the military . . . Tony, I saw things, things that just shouldn't happen. The world is in too much pain. That pain seeped into my heart, and I lost my way. Standing behind a bar was just less work. At least it used to be, before my body gave out." His boisterous laugh busted free again.

I don't know why Dennis laughed all the time. Was it because he just had a knack to find delight in all things? Or was it the opposite? Can laughter actually be a language of pain, a momentary explosion of soul release? In Dennis's case, I wondered if it was the latter.

Back to our conversation under the East India Company sign, I answered his question about my work. "Dennis, to tell you the truth, I am thinking about getting out of the game."

"What does that mean?"

I had my old briar pipe in my hand. I tamped away inside the bowl, watching the thin string of smoke, and pondered my response. "You know that I have been struggling with my faith for the past few years. But now things feel pretty good. I have found a simpler and quieter version of faith, and God is more accessible to me now than he ever was before. I spent ten years of my life as a mercenary for God, and I am tired. I don't necessarily want to quit. I just want to rest."

"Mercenary, huh? That's a pretty strong word. Did God tell you to be a mercenary?"

I think it is a bartender trick. You don't really say anything at all. You just restate what the other person says in the form of a question to keep the other person talking.

"Well, no, God did not ask me to be a mercenary. That is just where I ended up, a hired gun in the army of God."

Dennis thought about my words for a moment, then said, "I didn't know that God had an army." He took another drink. "I actually know what it is like to be a hired gun, to be sent to foreign lands without a say in the matter and to see horrifying things."

Dennis continued, pointing his words at me. "Tony, I see the spark of God inside you. Someone needs to tell you that. I don't know why your religious friends aren't saying it to you, but I will. I haven't been to church in decades (God have mercy), but still I can see the spark inside you."

I wasn't used to people talking to me like that. Affirmations of my spirit had been rare in recent years. Out of reflex, I changed the subject. I asked Dennis about his other interests. He is at an age where he should start to think about retirement, and though I didn't want to bring it up, I knew his body would not allow him to tend bar too much longer. "So, do you have a plan for life after the Horse Brass?"

Boisterous laugh. "At this point I am just an ole bartender. That's what I am. As long as they let me work, you will find me right here, standing behind that bar." He pointed over his shoulder at the long, carved bar behind him, now tended by Arthur.

He played with the beer in his pint while he talked. He swirled it around in the glass like a wine connoisseur. I assumed he was looking into his ale for magical insights: color, clarity, carbonation. Or maybe it was his crystal ball. "Tony, when I was a boy, I believed that I had the call. I never told anyone about it, but I believed that I was supposed to be a priest. Somewhere along the line, I lost my way and God took his call away from me. I know that I let him down." Dennis is a big, softhearted old soul. As he spoke, his eyes filled with tears and his head bowed in shame. "I just hope that when this life is over, God will still want me with him."

My eyes, my mind, my heart, and my soul were all fixed on my sweet bartender friend. He hid nothing from me, and I loved him for it.

Once the fog of his emotions had past, he looked me in the eye and said, "I don't know what you are supposed to do with your life, but take it from someone who knows regrets: don't get out of the game. Leave that mercenary crap behind. Stay in and find another way to play."

I looked at him, with my heart full of affection. I knew he was right. "I don't know how else to play." But I committed in my heart, *I will try to stay available to God. I will try to play in a different way.*

———

It has been ten years since those conversations. I don't visit the Horse Brass much these days. Around this time, Aimee and I got married and a few years later started making babies. I struggled leaving the pub life behind even though I knew it wasn't best anymore to lose long hours every week holed away in an east Portland bar. Life evolves. I evolved. But I still miss the crew from the pit. I miss the darts. I miss the unstructured conversations among friends, wandering in a field of discovery.

At the Horse Brass, voices like Katarina's helped me heal from my yesterdays, ragamuffins like Pope healed my ever-changing todays, and Dennis helped me move into my tomorrows with a belief that the God-life could be something other than mercenary. Hope returned. It often felt weak, but sometimes you only need a seed of hope to plant.

So, I decided to stay in the game. I tried to see each new opportunity through new eyes, free of violence, full of love. I looked for opportunities not to fight for God, but to walk with him. I began to believe that God was the one who was creatively tilling, planting, and harvesting all around me. The joy was to take his hand as he led me into his eternal play of love.

So, like a walk in the cool of the day, God led me to a new garden to explore.

LEARNING TO REED

YOU ARE ABOUT TO ENTER A PLACE THAT IS SACRED TO ME. REED College is among the most interesting institutions of learning anywhere in the world. The campus has also been much maligned in many circles. The stereotypes are many, some of which are addressed through the experiences in these next chapters. Stereotypes are never fair. I pray you can see past the stereotypes. I hope you can see, through my eyes, the tremendous beauty that Reed releases in the lives of its students . . . and in me.

14

EDEN

I BUMPED INTO AN OLD COLLEGE BUDDY AT A PARTY. HIS CHOSEN occupation was professional minister. After a little small talk, he shared with me some of his plans.

"I am thinking about being a missionary to Reed College. What do you think about that?" As he said it, he lightly punched me in the shoulder.

It was clear that he expected me to be impressed by his great faith. I also felt like I was supposed to be nervous for him, as if he were planning to go off to war. What was it about Reed College that made my friend talk this way? Why did he expect his declaration to surface such strong emotions in me?

It ended up being just talk. He never even visited Reed's campus.

I had heard the legends of Reed College. It was the sort of place that pastors use in sermon illustrations, in the same category as North Korea or the red-light district. I had been warned by religious folk not to visit there. "Reed College is the most pagan place in the city." "Don't go without your spiritual armor securely fastened." "It is a training ground for the liberal elite, like a secret society." "Reed is barely a college; it is just a front to disguise darkness and debauchery."

It sounds kind of cool, doesn't it?

My phone rang. It was Allan.

I wish you could meet Allan. He is a wonderful man.

Allan is the last man in America who wears suspenders every day, regardless of his outfit . . . and somehow he makes it work.

Allan had an unusual request. "Tony, I need to ask a favor of you." Allan has a salt-of-the-earth pragmatism about him. His conversations are straight to the point.

"Name it," I answered without pause. Allan had always been a loyal and supportive friend to me, and there was almost nothing he could ask that I would not gladly do for him.

I could tell that he felt bad about inconveniencing me. "Would you be willing to befriend a freshman at Reed College? His name is Mitch. He studies physics." Allan went on to explain that he had been asked by an old friend to contact Mitch. For some unspoken reason, Allan did not feel comfortable fulfilling the request. He wasn't sure what to do and wanted to pass the request on to me. "Would you be willing to give him a call? Maybe buy him a cup of coffee? I am sorry to bother you. I didn't know who else to ask." Before I could respond, he finished with, "He is spiritually lonely. He may be the only Christian on that entire campus."

I told him I would give Mitch a call.

After I hung up, I thought about Allan's last statement: "He may be the only Christian on that entire campus." That was an odd thing to say, especially considering there are more than fourteen hundred students at Reed College. However, as weird as it sounded, it did not completely surprise me. It was typical of how Christians spoke about Reed.

Personally, I wasn't sure what to think about the southeast Portland college. I had never known anyone who had attended Reed. Neither had I known any member of her faculty or staff. Ironically, at that time, I lived only a mile from the campus, but I had never entered her buildings or walked her tree-lined paths.

In light of everything I had heard, my general thought was, *Why would I go there?* I had been taught that there was only one reason a Christian visits Reed College. A Christian only goes to Reed if he wants to "test his faith."

My faith-testing days were long behind me.

———

Many months later, after embedding myself in the Reed world, I would find myself chuckling at the Christians who would come to the campus on spiritual safari. They would stand out like tourists on the savanna, walking about in their khakis and pressed button-downs, snapping mental pictures of all the wild pagans.

Eventually I learned that Reed was not a place to test your faith at all; it is a place to inspire your faith.

———

I first met Mitch on a Monday afternoon.

Reed is located in a sequestered section of southeast Portland on a hundred parklike acres. It is on the edge of one of Portland's most opulent neighborhoods. The city's thoroughfares steer far around her. Most people drive through Portland without any idea of where exactly Reed is. I wonder if they like it that way.

To stumble upon the campus is to be inspired. In a way, it is a place deserving of legends. Fortresslike brick buildings sit far off the road. Hundred-year-old trees provide her outer defenses.

I wove through narrow neighborhood streets and finally turned onto Woodstock. As I approached, my imagination drifted. I tried to imagine what this legend-college would be like up close.

I parked in an adjacent neighborhood. I found a spot about a block from the campus border and about three blocks from her closest building. I foolishly assumed that Reed controlled parking on campus the way all other universities do. Of course, I was wrong. Without permission or permit, I could have parked anywhere I liked. It was the first of her many unexpected freedoms.

I trudged across the wide lawn toward a cluster of buildings at the west end of the campus. I had a vague sense of where to find the student commons. After walking through a grove of maples and one wise old sycamore, I entered through a tunnel under a three-story brick dorm-block with iron lamps and the number 1912 stamped in the gray stone above the arch.

I left the sunlight behind and climbed into the ten-foot-wide rabbit hole with no idea how "deep" this rabbit hole went or what world lay on the other side.

Out of the arched darkness and back into the sunlight I found myself in a broad jousting arena. Well, not exactly, but that is how I imagined it. There was a tall, brick fortress all around. The courtyard was long and narrow, approximately 150 yards long and 70 across. I envisioned it as the perfect setting for snorting steeds of sport and ironclad combatants.

My imagination was filled with drama, but reality was far more peaceful. Students sat all around in small groups, some on the lawn, others at small tables. Peaceful, yes . . . but I could not shake the thought that they were all staring at me. Did they know I wasn't one of them? I felt as though I was wearing knee-high argyle socks,

Bermuda shorts, a fedora, and pink sunblock on my nose. I was a fool walking through someone else's dream. I didn't belong. So, I increased my pace and leaned toward the glass doors on the courtyard's other side.

I kept my eyes low. I tried not to draw attention to myself.

Luckily the student commons was easy to find, and Mitch seemed to have no problem picking me out of the throngs of students coming and going. (I wonder how. Was it my Bermuda shorts?)

Thank the Lord for Mitch. I was relieved not to be alone. I looked around the grand room full of students and silently declared, *I am Mitch's friend! I belong because I am with Mitch.* It is amazing how just one person can bring belonging.

We grabbed a cup of coffee and sat down to get to know each other. Mitch chose a table at the room's center. I would have chosen a discreet table at the vaulted room's perimeter, near the windows. I was "Mitch's friend," however, and Mitch got to call the shots.

Mitch was a delight. He wore glasses similar to those my grandfather wore: simple wire rims. Mitch was most comfortable in jeans and a fleece pullover. Though only eighteen years old, he was already twice as smart as I had ever been and twice as secure in his opinions as I could ever hope to be.

This is the part of the story where I am supposed to retell the stimulating details of our first exchange. I wish I could. The truth is, I didn't understand much of it, and the parts I did understand long ago slipped from my memory. All I remember was my desperate attempt to mentally keep up. I also remember that my head hurt when we were done.

In time, like all cultural transitions, this foreign experience soon became commonplace. The headaches eased. And like being pulled behind a ski boat, all you can do is relax and enjoy the ride.

Mitch was my teacher in the "Gospel According to Einstein." And I tried to be a good follower.

My memories of those early weeks with Mitch are filled with con-versations about Jesus and physics. Every question had a physics answer. Be it quarks or quantum mechanics, Mitch had a scientific metaphor for any spiritual idea. Every once in a while I understood exactly what he was talking about. On second thought, that is probably a lie. I never *really* understood.

Through those Monday afternoons with Mitch, my circle of Reed friendships slowly grew. Each new friend was similarly impres-sive, only varying in language. Some spoke history; others, biology or French literature. Each new friend was striking and stimulating.

If I could recall every detail, I am sure that I expressed plenty of opinions, but that is not the part I remember. What I do recall is asking questions and then shutting up and letting my new friends talk: "What are your dreams for this world? What do you think makes existence meaningful? What makes someone a good per-son? What do you think God is like? Where have we gone terribly wrong?" These kids were thoughtful and verbose. Regardless of the topic, there were sides to be taken, positions to be defended, and arguments to be made. They played off one another like a game of Hacky Sack. I was honored just to be included in the circle.

Within a couple of months I was no longer an outsider invading someone else's dream sequence.

I had become a part of their dream, and they had become part of mine.

The Bible says that God put the very first humans in a garden full of trees, called Eden. From the language, it would seem that this garden was the very definition of freedom and exploration. Moses wrote,

"The LORD God made all kinds of trees grow out of the ground—trees that were pleasing to the eye and good for food." And God said to the first man and woman, "I give you every seed-bearing plant on the face of the whole earth and every tree that has fruit with seed in it. They will be yours for food." This first garden was clearly intended to be a place of discovery, a place to explore. It was a place where God walked in the cool of the day and where his human friends were invited to walk with him.

Reed is like Eden. That may seem like a strange statement. I am not saying that it is a total parallel, but it is similar. Like Eden, it is also a beautiful garden of trees, more trees than I could ever name: Alaska-cedar and California Bay, Chinese Elm and Japanese snowbell, black locust and coast redwood; ash to Zelkova; walnut, plum, lime, pear, apple, and cherry. It is a garden, a set-aside place, where freedom, discovery, and exploration are vigorously encouraged. Ironically, it is also a place where you may see someone walking around as naked as Adam.

In the theme of Eden, Reed quickly became one of the garden spots in my story. I am not saying that it was safe or comfortable. It was quite the opposite. The philosophy of life and the veracity of the students put my life on alert. Words were no longer flippant things to be tossed around without sober consideration. I witnessed how words become thoughts, and thoughts become beliefs, and beliefs become passions, and passions become the music by which we live.

The Reed culture was stimulating and meaningful, and (I am not sure how else to say this) it was a place that I felt God had prepared just for me. It was the natural destination of my life up to that point. For that I am eternally grateful.

Monday afternoons soon grew into most every afternoon of the week. In time I audited a class or two to further stretch my mind. Soon, I invited my friend Don, a local author and kindred spirit, to come hang out with me on campus. The two of us walked the garden of Reed together.

In the garden of Eden, freedom reigned. Every plant and animal companion was the unqualified delight of God's flesh-friends. There was only one thing forbidden, a single tree that God asked his flesh-friends not to eat. It was called the Tree of Knowledge of Good and Evil.

Reed students also understand a profound sort of freedom. Reedies are uniquely released to walk their academic garden and feast from any philosophical fruit. Before I arrived, I was taught that Reed also had a single forbidden fruit: Christianity. At least that was what the legends claimed.

Many legends are based in truth; others are not. Over the next couple of years, I set out to discover if this particular legend was indeed based in truth . . . or did it sprout from lies?

15

SAINTS

THE LEGENDS I'D HEARD ABOUT REED COLLEGE WERE NOT WITH-
out statistical support. The year I met Mitch, *Princeton Review* declared
Reed the least religious college in America.

Princeton Review provides a funky survey system of America's
colleges and universities. Almost four hundred colleges are polled
each year regarding a whole buffet of topics. When all the "religious" questions are tallied, Reed always ends up at the bottom of
the god-pile.

Many Reedies take a certain pride in this ranking.

Many religious people use this ranking as proof that Reed students hate Christians. Based on the legends, I also suspected this
was true.

There is no place I have ever been, be it Albania or a Manhattan
homeless shelter, where I felt more uncomfortable and self-conscious
than at Reed. I can only guess why that was.

My father had always been the smartest man in any room he

walked into. That is a challenging example to live up to. Maybe I believed that I needed to be as smart as him, which was a lost cause at Reed.

This sense of discomfort is why it was such a relief to meet Saint Michael.

Saint Michael had been a ten-year fixture around Reed's campus.

It took no time for Saint Michael and me to discover each other. We were similar. We were both in our early thirties, and we were also "outsiders," meaning we were not students. We both had a real love for Reed culture. The difference between us was he had been at Reed long enough to be fully comfortable in her academic and relational gardens.

Saint Michael was also a Jesus guy.

Truth be told, my time at Reed might have been a mere commercial break in my story if it weren't for Saint Michael. From the first moment we met, he believed that I was made for Reed College. He would repeatedly affirm this belief . . . and that meant something. He had given a decade of his life to loving a place that 99 percent of Christians missed. Saint Michael believed I was different. He believed that I would not miss it either.

My life overlapped with Saint Michael's for only a few short months.

Life is most challenging when one set of affections collides with another. Within three months of my arrival at Reed, Saint Michael had just such a collision. A family crisis required him to move out of state. Reed obviously could not go with him, and he could not stay. He made the necessary and heroic decision to serve his family. After ten years, he left Reed behind.

But before he moved, Saint Michael asked me to meet him at Papaccinos coffeehouse.

When I arrived at the coffeehouse, Michael was visibly sad. I sat down across from him in a matching wingback chair next to the front window. He played with his herbal tea in an oversized teacup.

He told me the story of his family's crisis and explained his need to move. Then he begged me to remain at Reed as long as I could. He said that it would make it more bearable for him to leave if he knew I would stay. To him, the request was sacred. I understood it as such.

How could I deny a sacred request?

During that first spring term, a few months before our meeting at Papaccino's, Saint Michael helped concoct a plan. It was an idea that he was convinced was perfect for Reed. John Perkins, the renowned civil rights leader, was coming to town for a series of lectures. Michael worked hand in hand with Reed's administration to add the campus to Dr. Perkins's demanding speaking schedule. He was going to speak in the campus's largest venue, Kaul Auditorium.

Michael explained to me, "John Perkins is a true national treasure. He is one of the remaining leaders of the American civil rights movement. He worked alongside Martin Luther King Jr. He has labored for decades in the American South for civil equality, racial reconciliation, and social justice."

I understood his enthusiasm. I was even caught up in it. But I could not deny my doubts. "I get everything you are saying, Michael. But isn't he also a Southern pastor? He is a Bible-preaching Jesus guy. I mean, I don't know a ton about him, but I do know that. Are you sure this is a good idea?"

Saint Michael took my hesitations to heart. He said, "There are not very many things that I am *sure* of these days. I do know that Dr. Perkins will bless the campus just by being here. Now . . . will he be received? That is up to the students." Then he added, "Tony, you need to be careful about jumping to conclusions. These students will surprise you. Don't judge them so quickly."

I appreciated what Saint Michael was trying to accomplish. Though I questioned his wisdom, by faith I tried to mirror Michael's sense of expectation.

———

The night Dr. Perkins came, I slipped past the coat-check window and through the large foyer into Kaul Auditorium. I was early. I climbed the ascending stairs and took a seat along the north wall, halfway to the back. The auditorium is large for a small college like Reed and is the regular venue for popular events like traveling orchestras or the Portland Gay Symphonic Band. My eyes wandered around the mostly empty cavern and across the hundreds of empty seats.

I wondered how many students would come. This is Reed College, after all. It was a midweek evening lecture placed in the middle of prime study hours, featuring a speaker whom I imagine none of them had heard of. I was concerned. I closed my eyes. Regardless of how many (or few) did come, I tried to imagine how they would receive Dr. Perkins.

At ten minutes to seven, a steady stream of students began to enter. The stream grew into a river. Within fifteen minutes the room was filled.

It was quite a crowd. My eyes absorbed the growing numbers. The best way to describe the room would be a cross between any American college campus (concert T-shirts, a guy in an Indianapolis Colts jersey, and a lot of denim) and a gypsy camp (bright natural fibers, scarves, electric-purple hair, and dreadlocks).

Everyone took their seats and waited. A din of expectation hung over the room.

A few minutes later a student named Nadine climbed the stairs and took her place behind the unassuming podium at the center of the wide stage. Nadine is the very definition of elegance, and she conferred that elegance to the entire auditorium.

Nadine introduced Dr. Perkins without fanfare. Her words were simple and without flourish. That was Dr. Perkins's wish.

The old man, already in his seventies, slowly rose from his seat. He moved deliberately. He carefully climbed the stairs and took his place behind the small podium. He looked over the room. He is not a large man, stooped further with age. He wore a simple suit, and large glasses rested on his dark face. Four hundred young faces stared back at him.

Though he had personally advised five presidents, addressed Congress, and spoken to audiences of thousands, you would have thought this was the most significant group he had ever spoken to. He humbly thanked Nadine. Then he thanked the room, moved that they would show him such honor and give him the gift of their time. He greeted them on behalf of his family and his community back home in Mendenhall. He closed the introduction by saying, "I greet you in the name of our Lord Jesus Christ."

His address lasted forty-five minutes. I looked around. No one moved.

With his simple Southern accent, he set the stage of racial and economic injustice in America. He began with his childhood and walked the room through the essential and painful drama of the 1960s. He unapologetically insisted that the disparities of race and class remain today.

Dr. Perkins spoke of his own personal story in the broader civil rights narrative. He spoke about his family. He talked about the death of his brother Clyde at the hands of police. He spoke of his numerous nonviolent stands, many of which ended in his imprisonment, alongside his family and friends.

With the stage of the civil rights story carefully set, he then told a story of one of his arrests. He described being thrown into a police station's windowless back room. He was crumpled to the floor under a surround of large, white police officers. His voice was clear and deliberate, steeped in his Mississippi accent. While he spoke, he made every effort to make eye contact with each student. "I was without defense as they beat me," he recalled. "I can remember seeing my own blood splatter on the wall as they struck me again and again."

Then he paused. The room was silent. His words continued. "As I lay there at the feet of those huge, white police officers, I looked up into their faces . . . twisted with anger . . . immediately my heart was filled with compassion. Seeing them, all I could think was, *Dear Jesus, what pain these men must have endured in their lives to feel such hatred. Have mercy on them.*"

You could have heard a moth's wings.

He allowed the moment to wash over the room.

From there Dr. Perkins moved to his own thoughts on the very real plight of America's disenfranchised and marginalized communities. He expressed how these populations have been systematically removed from the national consciousness, and affirmed the absolute need for a new generation, one fueled by compassion and a sacrificial life.

And then he stopped.

You could tell the speech was almost over, but not quite. He took off his glasses and stared out over the podium, looking back and forth across the student gathering. "There is one more thing." He pointed his glasses at the room, not in a menacing or demanding way, but like a grandfather imparting his most crystallized wisdom after a long, hard life. "There is no hope." He paused and gestured with his glasses again. His eyes squinted as if he was straining to be sure that every ear was listening. "There is . . . no . . . hope apart from the reconciling work of Jesus Christ.

There is no hope apart from a revival of God's love across this country. There is no hope for our broken communities apart from the cross of Jesus Christ and his resurrection. There is no hope to reverse the tide of racism. There is no hope to heal poverty and return dignity to all people. There is no hope for my people back in Mendenhall, and there is no hope for you and your people here at Reed College. The gospel of Jesus Christ . . . he is our only hope." His glasses were now held high. He continued to squint. Then he returned the glasses to their place atop his nose and finished with a simple, "Thank you."

And with that, he stepped away from the podium and moved toward the stairs.

That is when it happened.

Like a sonic boom, four hundred students rose to their feet and filled the echoing space with applause. There was no hesitancy. With a choreographed conscience they stood tall, held their hands high, and applauded.

After several seconds there came the typical deadline when applause is supposed to dissipate. All of us are taught early in life the approved life span of applause. These students ripped through that deadline. Then they ripped through the next. They had no respect for protocol. Ten seconds turned to thirty. One minute turned to two. Time stopped, and those students stood and honored a man, his message, and a life well lived. The ruckus rose and rose.

———

I have never gotten over that evening in Kaul Auditorium with Dr. Perkins. It was that night that I finally understood that the legends about Reed College contained lies, preposterous lies. Reed students don't hate Christians. I sat and watched them honor and even express love to an elderly man who was possibly the most forcefully outspoken Christian to ever walk onto their campus. They didn't hate the gospel of Jesus. No one could have preached it more clearly than they had heard it that night.

Jesus said, "Woe to you, teachers of the law and Pharisees, you hypocrites! You are like whitewashed tombs, which look beautiful on the outside but on the inside are full of dead men's bones and everything unclean."

Reedies want the same thing that Jesus wants. They want authenticity, not hypocrisy. They want faith that leads to activism, not institutionalism. They want to believe in something not because it is redundantly preached but because it is sacrificially lived.

That night with Dr. Perkins was the first of so many experiences around faith that I spent sitting alongside Reed students. Over the months that followed, I watched a new set of beliefs rise like a creation chorus:

We Believe

We believe in a faith that is marked by personal transformation
We believe in a faith that is not fueled by a self-serving agenda
We believe in a faith that is as true in actions as in words
We believe in a faith that leads to a haggard life
We believe in a faith that happens in dialogue, not monologue
We believe in a faith that experiences poverty for the other
We believe in a faith that joins the marginalized
We believe in a faith that transforms communities as well as individuals
We believe in a faith that exists for the poor as well as the rich
We believe in a faith that is for the forgotten as well as the popular

*We believe in a faith that is for the anonymous as well as
the famous
We believe in a faith that is for the beaten as well as the
abuser
We believe in a faith that brings hope*

Certainly this creed does not tell the whole story; no creed ever does. These beliefs do, however, sound an awful lot like Dr. Perkins. They sound a lot like Jesus.

———

Saint Michael had been right, and thank goodness he was. Not only had Dr. Perkins's visit not been a mistake; that night proved to be life changing . . . for me, at least, if not also for another four hundred souls.

A couple of months later, Saint Michael was gone. He had moved out of state. I missed his acceptance. I missed his guidance. I missed his friendship. His request that I would remain at Reed resonated in my heart. I prayed that I would not miss the life-altering gift of his sacred invitation.

16

ORDAINED

FOR MORE THAN TEN YEARS, SAINT MICHAEL HAD PERFORMED THE role of volunteer chaplain around Reed College. Each year he had mentored the handful of Jesus-students. He had led small Bible gatherings. He had tried to be the living presence of the supernatural wonder that Jesus called "the gospel." He had done it all deftly and with a light and respectful hand.

In his absence I wanted to honor his legacy and learn to love Reed students well, as he had.

Yet, it was clear to me that everything I had learned from my ten years as a professional Christian needed to be reformed, reframed, and rethought. Over the years, I had attended countless conferences and collected a library of instructional manuals. All those training folders, complete with colored tabs and marketing-speak, were thrown out the window. The traditional and "proven" structures were created for another place. It was terrifying to me to leave those safe formulas behind, but I had to. This was a brand-new garden.

=

The first week of the new semester, I was introduced to Jared. Jared was a graduate student at Reed. He was new just like me. We met through a mutual friend named Joshua, a crazy-haired theologian/ songwriter, who also happened to live in my basement. At Joshua's encouragement, I called Jared and asked if he wanted to grab some lunch. He agreed.

We met at Nicholas Lebanese restaurant.

Nicholas is like the glorious reward at the end of a treasure hunt. Most people don't even know it is there. It is an unbranded nook, sunk between large, outdated retail spaces along Grand Avenue. Only locals eat there. There is almost always a line.

The entire dining room is no larger than a small bedroom. There are twenty tables wedged into the quaint space. While dining, it is normal to bump shoulders with a stranger at an adjacent table (which inevitably leads to conversation, and if lightning strikes, friendship happens, even if it lasts only a lunch).

When I visit Nicholas, my favorite moment is when the waiter brings a manhole-sized pita bread, hot from the oven, and places it at the center of the table. It rests on a small metal scaffold the size of a top hat. On a winter day you can warm your hands over its steaming surface.

Jared and I arrived at the same time. We met at an off-hour and were therefore able to immediately get a table (a rare treat). We sat across from each other, leaning over the small table, our foreheads no more than twenty-four inches apart.

I was waiting for the pita.

Jared jumped in without the normal new-friend pleasantries. "Before the waiter gets here, there is something that I need to say."

"Okay. Go ahead," I responded. I was curious and also put off by his break from social norms.

Jared is a handsome guy with blond hair, a neatly kept beard, and intense blue eyes. I guessed he was in his midtwenties.

"Before we go through the whole process of eating lunch together and sharing our stories"—there was a flash of disappointment on his face; I suspect because he thought the phrase "sharing our stories" had become cliché "and before we start pretending like we are going to be friends, and before we talk about Reed College . . . or anything else, for that matter . . . there is something that I need to know from you."

Jared was clearly setting a tone. This was a line-in-the-sand conversation. I knew it, and he knew I knew it. Because of that, I liked him immediately. And I thought, *What drives this guy . . . and what on earth could be so important?*

Relieving my curiosity, he said, "The thing I need to know from you is this . . . Can you learn from a college student?"

I could not have predicted that one. It was an odd question, to be sure, and a particularly odd question to begin a friendship. I was intrigued and confused. "What do you mean?"

"Look: I grew up going to church. I have been a part of Christian groups, and I have known many pastors. One consistent truth from my experiences is the total inability of Christian leaders to learn from their subordinates. That is the sort of religious garbage I am not willing to put up with anymore. So, I ask you again: Before we consider having lunch, are you able to learn from a student? Can you learn from a student like me?"

Jared stared at me, waiting for me to respond. He was not joking, and I felt no humor in my soul. I searched my heart for the most honest answer. I knew I could not bluff him. I knew I had to tell the truth, my heart truth.

"Jared, I think your question is a reasonable one." I rubbed the bridge of my nose between my left thumb and index finger as I searched for the right words. "Listen . . . I can't speak for the pastors you have known. I wouldn't try. But I can speak for me. To be honest, I have all the tools for organizational abuse. I am tall. I am male. I am reasonably articulate. I am older than you. Everywhere I go, I am always one of the largest personalities in any room. And I have spent much of my life in the role of 'leader,' particularly in religious contexts. All these factors and more make me someone that you *should* be suspicious of."

I searched Jared's face to see if my words were connecting at all. He just sat, unmoved, eyes fixed. I wasn't sure what that meant, so I decided to keep talking. "The odds are that if you and I start to spend time together in any sort of group capacity, I am going to let you down. It is also safe to assume that there will be times when I will not learn from you, when I should just shut up and listen . . . but I won't . . . and it will be to my detriment." This sort of confession seemed to soften Jared. It even allowed a hue of amusement to leak onto his face.

I relaxed a bit and finished. "Here is what I can tell you. I have been kicked in the gut quite a few times in my life. I have known failure. I have known shame. And whether or not I do it consistently, I want to live as a learner. I want to live with the posture that any and every person is my teacher. My hope is that you can believe that and we can have a relationship of genuine exchange. Beyond that, I don't know what else to say."

Jared smiled.

Serendipitously, the waiter also arrived.

Jared looked at the waiter. Then he looked back down at me. I kept my eyes on Jared. I wondered if we were going to have lunch or go our separate ways.

Jared finally let me off the hook. "Well then, do you know what you want to order?"

"Could we start with some of that pita bread?"

—————

I quickly learned that Jared was what I might call a de-Christian. What I mean by that is he had spent much of his life in the Christian church, but now stood several steps outside her doors and for the most part was searching for a different faith home.

There were quite a few de Christians around Reed College. They had spent some season of their lives within a church context, but now felt little to no need for it. Many of them felt the experience around Christians was heavy-handed. Others felt there was not room for free exchange. Others were disappointed by the insecurity or the elitism they had experienced in church contexts. Whatever it was, they had, at some point along the way, climbed on a boat and set sail away from the island of Christendom. They were looking for a faith that was congruent. They wanted something they could live by.

I don't know if Jared's question surprised you as much as it surprised me. It absolutely surprised me. Later though, upon reflection, I concluded that Jared was onto something. And that something was quite important.

———

When I was in junior high, I was first exposed to evolutionary theory. It was required for all students. In my particular town there was no uproar about the need to also teach creation theory alongside evolution theory. In my town, that was a ridiculous idea. Evolution was the only reasonable curriculum.

One of the first ideas they taught us about evolutionary theory, in order to lay the foundation for survival of the fittest and other doctrines, was the idea of the food chain (it was just junior high, after all). The food chain was a simple idea: in every creature relationship there is the eater and there is the food. With some creatures you may be the eater, but with others you may be food—unless, of course, you happen to find yourself at the top of the food chain: a place of godlike power. When a lion meets an antelope, there is no role confusion. There is no need for the two beasts to draw straws or play "Eeny, meany, miny, moe." The lion is the eater and the antelope is the food. There is no discussion to be had on this matter. It is a ridiculous idea to conceive of the antelope eating the lion. Just try to picture it. It is like a panel from the newspaper cartoon. Consumption travels only one way.

Jared was illuminating that we often treat spiritual relationships with just such an evolutionary model. In church culture, I had been taught to position myself within a relational food chain. There are some relationships where I am the teacher (eater), and there are some relationships where I am the student (food). This spiritual ecosystem was clear and absolute. I was taught that it was essential. I learned to find my place in the pecking order.

Jared was tired of the pecking order. He was tired of being food; more specifically he was tired of the eater/food paradigm in spiritual relationships.

———

Over the weeks and months and even years to come, Jared and I became friends—which is astonishing. It is astonishing because Jared is arrogant. He is almost as arrogant as I am. In spite of these incontestable truths, in time we became more than friends; we grew to love each other. After our time at Reed came to an end, a few years later, we became struggling business partners and every once in a while even managed to pay our bills. In the midst of our struggle or success, we spent every day bantering about life, faith, purpose, meaning, and hope for a better world. Each topic offered a fresh dynamic where each of us had unique experiences to share or exclusive knowledge to offer. Regardless of those distinctives, we fought for an egalitarian exchange. We fought for life together, fueled by love.

———

Thanks to my conversation with Jared that day and many other off-putting exchanges with Reed friends, I was repeatedly reminded of my arrogance. I was reminded of my potential to limit relationships and thus miss out on the undiscovered gift. I prayed I could heal from the hierarchical addictions of the spiritual ecosystem; it was just an illusion, after all. My longing to listen and learn increased.

Finally, I realized that even though it was terrifying, I could actually leave the safe religious formulas behind. I did not need a ministry manual to fulfill my promise to Saint Michael. The "manual" was all around me. It could be found in the collective experience and insights of the Reed community. If I was just patient enough to listen, in time the way of Jesus in this context would start to take form. I suspected that it would not look like a small-town Jesus-life. It would not look like a suburban Jesus-life. It would not even look like a state-college Jesus-life. It would need to be a Reed-shaped Jesus-life. And it would have to take shape in me . . . and in us.

One Bible translation describes the Jesus-life like this: "The Word became flesh and blood, and moved into the neighborhood." I wanted to follow Jesus' lead. On one hand it was terrifying; on the other hand it meant simply moving into the neighborhood.

17

ECCLESIASTES

ONE DAY, AS MITCH AND I WERE TALKING IN THE STUDENT COM-
mons, I looked over his shoulder at something that simply did not
compute.

Over near the dishwashing room was a long half wall, just tall
enough to make a comfortable place to rest your elbow. Students
stood on each side of the hip-high wall, chatting away. However,
none of the students leaned on the wall's smooth wooden surface.
They couldn't. The top of the wall was cluttered with partially eaten
meals on dinner plates.

At first I was confused. Why would students leave their plates
on the wall when the dish room was only a few steps away? Second,
why would the wall provide such a popular social oasis?

Then I saw it. It should have registered sooner, but it was simply
outside my expectations: The students were eating. They were graz-
ing from one plate to the next, picking and choosing from the scraps
of other students' discarded meals.

My first thought was, *Ewwww*. (That was pure gut response.)
I couldn't take my eyes away. It was like watching a car crash. You

want to look away, but somehow you can't. I can only imagine the look that was on my face, but Mitch didn't seem to notice. He was using salt and pepper shakers to explain the limitations of the second law of thermodynamics and its parallels to the spiritual life.

I did not know what to do with my emotions. Inside, I tried to quantify my reactions. For some reason, I was able to stomach those munching on a half-eaten plate of french fries. However, the student finishing up a bowl of cereal made me physically queasy. The fact that the food rested on the plate of a total stranger was somehow repulsive to me. I can't explain it. I was not proud of my response. How did they know the eating habits of the original consumer? How did they know that the food had not been maliciously tampered with? What if it belonged to a drooler? These were the honest thoughts that ran through my head. And what kind of grown man uses the word *drooler*?

———

Have you ever met a "freegan"? There is a large community of freegans in Portland. Freegans gather their food from free sources. Sometimes they take from fruit trees on public land. More often they collect discarded food from Dumpsters behind local grocery stores. The discoveries can be significant: fruits, vegetables, eggs, really almost anything. It is amazing the things folks will throw away in our disposable culture.

The motivation for freeganism is hope. It comes from a hope for a better world, to walk lightly upon the earth and limit consumerism. It is an art form. It is a lifestyle. I have friends who practice this life art. While I have never gone "Dumpster diving" myself, I have always respected those who do.

That afternoon with Mitch in the Reed commons, I was captivated. I had never witnessed freeganism practiced on such a local level. It was fascinating. And once I got past my own illogical queasiness, it was even inspiring.

———

Saint Michael was gone. I was now a part of the small student fellowship. That was a nice thought. It is nice to belong.

At first it was just a handful of students with a couple of us "outsiders" tagging along. The students wanted to build some group norms into our schedule, and I thought that was a good idea.

One day, early in the autumn semester, we sat down to discuss what regular activities would be helpful to our shared spiritual life and to the greater Reed culture. There were only eight of us.

To get the topic rolling, I suggested that we could host a Bible study. I thought, *That seems like a perfectly logical suggestion. We are all big fans of Jesus and to varying degrees we all call ourselves Christians. What could be better than a Bible study?*

The response to my suggestion was tepid at best.

I felt God's Spirit, like a whisper in my ear: *Remember the conversation with Jared . . . Remember your experience with Dr. Perkins . . . Remember . . . remember . . .*

Looking into the students' faces, it was clear my suggestion had missed. I tried again. "Sorry. Let me try that again. What do y'all think we should do?" I glanced at my buddy Don. He nodded at this. He knew this was a much better course of discussion.

The students looked at each other, and like corn kernels in a popcorn popper, bounced thoughts off one another. They explained how all Reed students received plenty of Bible in their schedule. Every first-year student had to read the Bible along with the other great texts of Western history. In fact, even the most antichurch Reed student read the Bible more than most churchgoing Bible-thumpers I knew.

Then they pointed out how students have ample opportunity

to discuss the Bible. Reed believes in a classical Western education coupled with interactive learning through small-group student conferences. These conferences placed a dozen students in a room to dissect the various texts, free of didactic control.

That was when Ivan suggested, "Maybe we can offer a different sort of interaction. We can open a space to personalize the questions of faith and spiritual devotion." He emphasized the word *personalize*.

This idea seemed to resonate with the students.

After fifteen minutes, and a few questions of clarification, it was agreed: Thursday evenings at seven o'clock we would hold a faith discussion. The goal would be to personalize the questions of faith.

Nadine reserved a classroom in the biology building, not far from the entrance to the campus library. That way the students could treat the discussion as a study break.

———

Later, I thought more about the discussion group idea. I thought it was a great idea. It was a brilliant marketing strategy. (This statement reveals that I still didn't get it.) I saw it as brilliant marketing because it embodied so many norms that the Reed students already bought into. It was philosophically driven. It followed the model of the school's small-group conferences. We would open the conversation to uncontrolled exchange, affirming the right to any position or opinion. All the while, we could slip little bits of Jesus-truth into every conversation. My mentality was like that of a man selling cleaning products door-to-door.

We planned out the semester. The students were happy to let Don and me participate and even facilitate some of the discussions (which was quite easy, because these students were so used to unbridled exchange). After a few weeks of trial and error, we laid out a series of questions to discuss, which included: What is God like? Why am I so screwed up? Why is the world so screwed up? What does it mean to be a "good" person? What made Jesus unique? Why is the cross such a powerful symbol in human history? What is the nature of religious devotion? What is conversion? Can I be spiritually free?

It was a ball.

I remember the week we discussed "Why am I so screwed up?" We were several weeks into the semester, and our small gathering had already grown to more than a dozen. I know that is not a huge number, but it felt significant to us. The most enjoyable part was the fact that only half the room would personally identify with the Christian belief system. We were a truly diverse crew.

"Tonight we are going to explore the question, why am I so screwed up?"

The conversation bounced around in rapid succession. We covered everything from the nature of morality, the relativity of goodness, the place of the will, personal responsibility, and the impact of one's cultural construct.

At one point in the conversation, we began to pass around a small, hardbound book from the Reed library's lower stacks. It was a typical book from an academic library. It had a solid royal blue cover. There were no words on the front, and the spine had only white letters stamped in a simple font: title, author, and reference number. It was a unique book. The pages contained no words, not one. Each page housed a single black-and-white photo. The topic: genocide. It was a photo essay of genocide on the African continent at the end of the twentieth century. The photos were graphic and gruesome, yet strangely dispassionate. Slaughtered bodies lay on every page. Many killed by machete. Many hacked to death by people they had known all their lives.

We passed the book around. The room was still. We sat together in that second-story classroom of the biology building; each soul denied the urge to look away. We were together in a holocaust museum. And each person present chose to enter the pain of our African neighbors across the globe.

Then the question was posed. "Ask yourself, 'Am I capable of this?'" A moment of pause and then, "If you had been born in these same circumstances, would you be capable of murder like this?"

Opinions again swirled, more slowly than before. There was more reflection and almost sacred consideration. Some insisted that they would never be able to hack another to death, especially someone they knew. Others in the group, with defeated tones, expressed only a wobbling hope that they were above such horrors.

In the end, Logan looked around the room. Logan was a third-year student with disheveled hair and a vintage wool sweater with holes worn through the elbows. He chose his words with care, as if discovering each one as he said it. "We are in an impossible quandary, aren't we?" He rubbed his fingers lightly on his forehead as he spoke. "Either we admit that we are capable—if we were subjected to the same cultural experiences as the murderers in these photos, we, too, would act in exactly the same way—or, on the other hand, we take the position that we are above such things. If we do, we suggest that we are fundamentally made of a morally superior material than our African neighbors, which is essentially the same argument that the Nazis used to justify the Aryan race." He looked genuinely horrified by his own realization. "Murderer or Nazi: if we are honest, humanity has been left with no choice."

I thought to myself, *That is quite possibly the best definition of human depravity I have ever heard.*

———

The weeks went by, and our Thursday evening conversations continued. The conversation rarely lasted more than an hour.

What I had originally thought was a great marketing strategy became a recondite experience that shaped the very way I believed. There were atheists, Buddhists, Jews, pagans, as well as folks from every point along the spectrum of Christianity, sharing openly about the ways of the spirit . . . and of God.

The roots of my faith sank deeper and deeper into Jesus through these conversations. These diverse perspectives, offering minerals of truth, nourished me. They also convinced me that while there is an ideology wrapped up around Jesus' life and teachings, ultimately Jesus is a person, a living presence. He was *with* us in those Thursday evening discussions. He joined us in the room. He was whispering into the ears of those present. And if I was willing to listen, I was often surprised how his thoughts came to light through their words.

The Reed students made such an experience possible. I learned from their insights. Even more, I learned from their attitudes, a delightful willingness to receive from the other.

I got to sit in the front row and watch them practice freedom and congruence in community. Back in the student commons, Reed students were free to eat off a stranger's plate amid a circle of social exchange because they long for a world with less waste.

Similarly, on Thursday evenings, Reed students were free to attend a meeting where friends gathered for a conversation that was heart-mined and true. They were free to open their own ideas and pain. They feasted on the ideas of others. They helped themselves to the philosophical plates around the room. They helped me become a faith freegan and to get over my queasiness and thankfully accept, even when the nourishment came off someone else's plate.

18

———

LESSONS

A LACK OF ANXIETY: THAT WAS ONE OF THE MOST LIFE-ALTERING aspects of life together among the Reed community. In particular, there was a lack of anxiety regarding topics of faith and religion.

Anxiety happens when my identity gets wrapped around an idea that is apart from me, something that feels out of my control. For me, deadlines in my work can lead to anxiety. Unreconciled relationships can also create anxiety. Money problems often surface a particularly fitful sort of anxiety. And interfaith dialogue can be a geyser of anxiety.

———

My father was not a chatty man. He believed in an economy of words, and he chose them carefully. I have very few memories of my father overtly mentoring my spirit. He did mentor me in a thousand covert ways: I watched him read his Bible every morning. I listened to him pray for our family before meals. I watched him steal away many, many nights to serve on church boards. I know he gave money to Christian causes.

The overt lessons, though, were few and far between . . . which is why this story made such an impact.

One day in particular my dad came home from work. I could not have been older than twelve. I remember the day so clearly because he went out of his way to initiate a conversation.

"Tony, I had an interesting interaction at work today."

I was surprised, expectant, and a little confused. I wanted to encourage him to continue. So I reached deep into my twelve-year-old vocabulary reservoir and responded with, "Uh-huh."

Dad took that as his cue to continue. "I don't know if you remember Bill; he works with me in my office. Bill is a Mormon. I don't know if you knew that . . . Anyway, today, I stopped by his office to check on something, and we got to talking . . . It started as a pleasant conversation. Then Bill surprised me by telling me that he had been hoping he and I could spend some more time together because we both go to church." Dad appeared to be searching for the best way to summarize Bill's words. "He said he wanted to talk about our beliefs sometime."

This topic was very exciting to me (despite the patented adolescent blank look on my face). Back in the '80s, there was a lot of talk at church about Mormons. In my church, Mormons were one of the chief bad guys. In truth, I didn't know much about them, but I did know that they were a cult . . . oh, and something about holy pajamas.

"What did you say?" I asked.

Dad looked me square in the eye. I knew it was one of those man-to-man moments, and we had not had many of those. "Tony, in light of the circumstances, I did what I had to do." His face was serious, if not stern. "I told him that there is nothing about his faith that I respect and that I was not interested in spending time together. I told him I was not and would never be interested in listening to him talk about his beliefs."

And with that, the lesson was over.

I knew I was supposed to take this as an important moment of training. I remember thinking how strong my dad was to speak with such boldness. His faith was strong.

That conversation happened thirty years ago, but I remember it clearly. It exists in my memory among my library of formative lessons that my dad gave me. Anyone who knew my dad will probably be surprised by this story.

I don't know what was going on in my dad's heart in regards to Bill or why he would go out of his way to teach me this lesson. I do know that this encounter produced tension in me in the area of faith exchange.

It taught me to distrust the other. It taught me to live with suspicion. It left me anxious.

This conversation with my father released a wave inside my soul that took almost thirty years to wash away.

The students at Reed helped push it back out to sea.

———

Any illusion that the community of Reed was perfect is exactly that: an illusion. We were deeply flawed and struggling to figure out how to live the life of faith in an unpredictably mixed community. We failed more than we succeeded. But we stayed in the questions, and that was the element that created the greatest hope.

The lack of anxiety around faith provided numerous paradigm shifts in my further understanding of the gospel.

Here are three more influential Reed experiences.

DENOMINATION

"Our fellowship needs a name."

The motivation was mostly pragmatic. After a while you can't keep describing yourself as "the Christian group, wherein many of the members are not Christians, and even those who are don't necessarily use the word *Christian*, and in fact, we have devoted participants who are clearly outside the Christian creed but still hold to Jesus as a formative and necessary voice in the dialogue of faith, purpose, earth, and meaning." I get tired just thinking it. You can see how this would be cumbersome.

As a result, we sought a congruent title that would adequately draw us all together. It needed to be true to our shared hope, without alienating our diverse collective. In the end, my friends SarrahLynne and Nadine made the most whimsical suggestion. "Why don't we call ourselves 'Oh for Christ's Sake'?"

It was brilliant!

What a thrilling and ironic title. Ultimately our diverse crew shared a single desire: to follow Jesus. This title blatantly embraced that hope. Simultaneously, this same title was playful, even amusing. To take an irreverent idiom and reverse it back on itself, to its truest meaning, was an act of delightful genius.

"Oh for Christ's Sake," or OFCS (what self-respecting organization can survive without at least one acronym), became the unifying canopy for our community's gatherings.

———

Before I ever got to campus, Ivan had a hobby. His hobby took place on Friday afternoons. The hobby was strangely simple. He took students to be with the homeless. To do that, he would check a van out from the Reed motor pool, park it at Eliot Circle, at the center of campus, and wait for students to arrive. Ivan did no publicity. And yet, eight to twenty students would show up every Friday afternoon to ride to a southeast Portland homeless shelter called St. Francis.

Ivan had no program. There was almost no plan. It was a simple ride. This ride offered only one promise: "You will get to spend two hours of your week with some of our neighbors who live outside." That was it. And yet despite its profound simplicity, students showed up every week. They showed up because a friend invited them. They showed up because they wanted to live out what they claimed to believe. They showed up because they cared.

I still remember the first time I met the van at Eliot Circle. I was there right on time, the same moment Ivan pulled the van around. At first it was just Ivan and me, leaning against the van under a canopy of Japanese Cherry trees. While I enjoyed a chance to stand and talk with my friend, for the most part I thought his little project was "cute," nothing more.

Then the students started to arrive. *Who are these people?* I thought. I had never met these students before. There were none of our usual Oh for Christ's Sake crowd.

Fascinating, I thought.

Within fifteen minutes there were fifteen students crammed inside the institutional passenger van.

Off we went to St. Francis.

After two hours of visiting, serving, and dining with several hundred outside-dwellers, Ivan gathered the crew back into the van, and we rumbled back to campus. All along the way we talked. While he drove, Ivan chummed the conversation. "Why did you come along today?" "What did you learn from our neighbors who live outside?" (Ivan was careful not to use terms like "homeless," which he believed could be a dehumanizing label.)

The conversation was electric. I could not help but think of Jesus' conversation where he stimulated others by saying, "As much as you have done it to the least of these, you have done it unto me."

Soon back on campus, the students piled back into their dorms, and the van was returned to the motor pool. That's when I jumped Ivan.

"Ivan, that was incredible! You provide this taxi ride to the homeless every Friday, and students just show up and come?" I was pretty amped up.

Ivan explained, "I have been doing this for over a year, and sometimes it is just six people, sometimes it is like today, but every week someone shows up."

"And you don't do any publicity?" My curiosity could not be contained.

"Nope, it's pretty much word of mouth, friends telling friends. I don't even invite people much anymore. It has taken on a life of its own."

I really wanted to encourage him. "Ivan, you need to know that this idea is really amazing. Not just the trip to St. Francis, but the *conversation* you led in the van on the way back. Brilliant! You are really illuminating the gospel of Jesus."

Ivan looked sheepish and a little confused. "I guess."

I didn't even notice Ivan's reticence. My desire to encourage could not be contained. "Ivan, I want to help you maximize the potential of this St. Francis thing. What if we called it the 'Oh for Christ's Sake Friday Homeless Outreach Project' and maybe make some fliers? The great part of this is not only would more people get exposed to St. Francis, not to mention your brilliant debrief questions, *but also* . . . students might be motivated to come to other OFCS events. It's called 'cross marketing.'"

Ivan looked at me like I was speaking Chinese. However, being the kindhearted gentleman he was, he was trying hard to hide his offense. "Tony, I provide the van for St. Francis so students can experience St. Francis and so they can be with people Jesus loves. I also do it for my fellow students, who I also love, so they can practice the things that we talk about in class."

Man, I love this kid. He is wonderful, though a bit naive. He was not quite catching my idea, so I explained more. "Ivan, I don't think you are listening to me. You and I are totally on the same wavelength here. We want the same thing, I just think you could expand your influence with a little advertising and some name recognition."

Ivan paused. Then he responded, trying to be respectful, "Tony, you are the one who is not listening. I don't want to expand influence. I understand your heart, but Jesus is perfectly capable of expanding his own influence. The Christian church has divided again and again over a need to brand their work. That is why there are hundreds if not thousands of denominations today. The reality is, St. Francis is doing beautiful things. Reed College is also doing a beautiful thing to let us use their van free of charge. Why on earth wouldn't we just support those two beautiful things without having to drape another name on top of it? Why turn it into a marketing strategy? At least, that is the way I see it."

I can be slow. I think I finally got the point.

As I drove home that day, I steeped in Ivan's words. "I don't want to expand influence . . . Jesus is perfectly capable of expanding his own influence . . . The Christian church has divided over the need to brand . . ." Round and round his words went inside me.

Why is it that every church needs its own homeless ministry, branded with the church's name? Or single mothers? Or recovery? Or school cleanup? Or, or, or, each branded with the church's marquee or specialized DBA.

Every neighborhood already has dedicated people and organizations in every realm of human need. What would happen if we stopped worrying about our religious brands? What would happen if we just supported those other dedicated souls with our time, talents, and money? What if we defended their efforts, not caring who gets the credit? How would that change the way others view the people of Jesus?

I think I know what Ivan would say.

I know what Jesus would say: "So when you give to the poor,

do not sound a trumpet before you, as the hypocrites do in the synagogues and in the streets, so that they may be honored by men. Truly I say to you, they have their reward in full."

HERESY

It was a spring afternoon. It was hard to believe that it was almost exactly a year after that first afternoon with Mitch in the student commons.

I got a phone call from Kym. The OFCS crew had returned to Portland a few days before from a delightful spring break adventure in the city of San Francisco.

Kym was also an "outsider" like me. She was a wonderful Christian woman. She loved to visit Reed College. Sometimes she would attend our Thursday discussion group or other gatherings. She wanted to encourage students in their faith, and for that I considered her a dear friend.

Over the phone, Kym asked if we could meet off campus at Papaccinos coffeehouse.

I agreed.

When I arrived, she was sitting at a semi-secluded table next to the mural-covered east wall. I waved to Kym and went to the bar and ordered my usual black coffee. It came in a cup the size of a soup bowl. (Hello!)

Armed with my auxiliary tank of caffeine, I took a seat across the table from Kym.

"Hey! How are you?" I was still emotionally intoxicated from the trip to San Francisco, and I'm sure it was written all over my face.

Kym responded in a reserved tone, which was not unusual in our interactions. "I am well. How are you? How was the trip?"

"The trip was great," I gushed. "There were eighteen of us. We crammed down there in a few cars. Half of us slept on floors.

Our friends in San Fran really hooked us up. Every day we got to serve in fascinating locations . . . Let's see . . . We spent one day in a shelter . . . another in a food bank, um, art projects in the Mission District, an elaborate lunch program in Golden Gate Park. Any single day could be considered life changing. Oh, and what a great crew: Penny, Nate, Ivan, Laura Jean, Jared, Mitch, and several students I did not even know before the trip started. And then there was—"

"I get it, I get it!" Kym abruptly stopped me mid-monologue. Her voice was uncharacteristically dramatic. She even drew a few looks from across the coffee shop. She was, of course, right to stop me. I had diarrhea of the mouth.

Kym took a moment to clear her throat. I could see she wanted to be clear and civil. "I have been watching you and the others for several months now. I want you to know that I have tried . . . *really* tried to be supportive in every way that I can. I applaud you for the conversations on Thursday evenings, chaotic though they may be." I could see that she was trying to ease into her point. "When I attended your prayer gathering . . . You must know, it is very difficult for me to remain silent when I hear several of the students' prayers where—oh, Lord, how do I say this?—when they obviously don't believe in the God of the Bible!"

It was clear to me that Kym was really upset and that her frustrations had been building for quite some time. I just sat and nodded. I wanted to give her as much time as possible to unload her burdening concerns.

She continued. "I was planning to keep quiet, just continue to pray about it, maybe talk to you during the summer, but I am afraid that I cannot hold back my thoughts any longer."

I wanted to set her at ease. "I am so glad that you didn't wait; please continue." There was a knot in my stomach. I kind of knew where her thoughts were going. Also, I hate criticism. And I wanted

Kym to like me. I wanted her to know that I liked her. These exchanges are never easy.

"Tony, when I heard about the trip to San Francisco, I knew that I could not wait any longer. I have to speak. Now, if I understand correctly, and please correct me if I am wrong, but several of the kids on this missions trip were not even Christians. Is that true?"

I responded shyly, "I imagine that, yes, yes, that is true."

"It is one thing to express creativity and openness around the Reed campus, even though it does put the Christian students at something of a risk, but when you go on a mission trip . . . !" The energy in her voice was increasing with each phrase. "The goal of a mission trip is to spread the love of Jesus and share the gospel. How can you possibly do that with any integrity if your ranks are full of people who don't even believe in Jesus?" Her voice spiked when she said "Jesus."

I searched her eyes. There was real turmoil there. I could see that she had been carrying this heavy load on our behalf. I can only imagine the depth and passion of her prayers for us over the week we had been gone.

"Kym, thank you for bringing this to me. I know that you love these students very much. I bet you were praying for us all during our trip. Is that true?

"Oh yes, yes, I was."

"I know. And you need to know that I believe that your prayers were one of the reasons why the trip was so spiritually significant. Not only did we participate in wonderful projects, serving others, but there is something else I want you to know. I believe that every student on the trip was truly enriched in their love for Jesus, those who call themselves Christians and those who don't."

I honestly don't know if Kym even heard what I said.

"Tony, I must tell you . . . you have to change the way you are leading this ministry."

At this, I had to respond. "I am not leading the ministry. The students are leading it. And ultimately I pray that God is leading it."

She let out a long exhale. "Okay!" She didn't want to lose her train of thought. "Over the past few months, I have listened to your words very carefully. Though your spiritual life is a little strange for my tastes, I don't doubt you believe all the essential things of the Christian faith, but these students . . . these students! What are you teaching them? You have to accept your greater responsibility."

I wanted her to get it all out. "What is it that you would like to see?"

"At some point you must separate out the Christian kids. They need to be built up in their faith. Where is the traditional Bible study? Where is the praise and worship?" Her passionate appeals flowed out in wave after wave, all laying the foundation for one crystallized point, the thing I knew was the reason for our coffee: "Tony, you are dangerous. You are hurting these kids. Someone has to say it. Your ways are too risky, and in fact they are destructive. Something has to change."

Her words broke against my soul like storm waves on the shore.

We spoke for almost an hour. I tried to listen and then tried to explain why we lived the way we lived. I wanted her to understand. I also wanted her to know that I, too, had had constant doubts. "This journey has been a terrible burden for me. Kym, I have laid in bed many nights aching over these very questions, begging God to help us."

In the end she confessed that she just could not stand by and watch us continue down this road. She apologized that she would not be able to support our events any longer and, in a spirit of honest disclosure, she confessed that she may need to help some of the Christian students find a *real* Christian fellowship.

When all the words had been spilt, I thanked her, shook her hand, and got up to leave.

It was a rainy spring afternoon. As I left through Papaccinos's glass door, I pulled my hood up over my bald head to protect it from the falling drops. I sank my hands deep into my jeans pockets and began the ten-block slog back to campus. I watched the lines on the sidewalk tick by under my steps. My thoughts bled. *Have we truly gone too far? Have I, through my voice or my silence, hurt these students I claim to love? Is it even possible to have a genuine community of Jesus-faith when the members are so diverse in beliefs?*

"Jesus, help us."

SALVATION

The months rolled by. Another spring pressed into a summer, and then the fall came once again. The school calendar reflects the ebb and flow of life: the "death" from good-byes to graduates and the "birth" from new students who would quickly become beloved friends.

Over those months and years, we processed the Scriptures together. This led to many long discussions and even more fresh discoveries. From classroom to the student commons, the eclectic musings poured. Through Old Testament and New, from Genesis to Revelation, it inspired and challenged us all. The conversations were not so much about which "team" one was on. They were more about how we should live and what we should love. The insights of these students from diverse backgrounds unearthed in me a broader and more inspiring view of the good news of Jesus than I had ever considered before.

Out of those lessons sprang these words. This was a view of biblical hope that all of us could passionately embrace. It was a hope we would proclaim to the world:

> *Imagine a world where there will be*
> *no more ethnic, cultural or racial hierarchy,*

*where slavery will be only a memory and with
no national prejudice or gender bias.*

*Imagine a world where there will be
no hunter and there will be no prey, where
the leopard will be the defender of the lamb
and the lion will eat grass.*

*Imagine a world where the
knowledge of God fills the earth and each
one marvels at the closeness of the Divine,
from the "least" to the "greatest."*

*Imagine a world where justice
always reigns, where the loving choice is
always made, where goodness flows like a river.*

*Imagine a world where there is no
more weeping or cries of distress, where all
children live beyond infancy and the old live
out their days.*

*Imagine a world where the poor do
not labor to benefit the rich, where those
who build houses live in them and all who
plant crops and vineyards enjoy them.*

*Imagine a world where people are not
oppressed and their lives and livelihood are
never taken from them.*

Imagine peace.

19

BENEDICTION

MY DAYS WALKING IN THE GARDEN OF REED COLLEGE CAME TO AN end much more abruptly than I would have hoped. The good-bye was unexpected and only partially my decision. There is pain there, to say the least—a pain that is still, in many ways, unresolved in my heart.

Before I tell you about the good-bye, though, there is one other thought I would like to share with you.

SUNSET

As a boy, I was taught the phrase "share the gospel." From my earliest days I knew this phrase and knew that it was an important if not essential part of the Jesus-life.

I heard this phrase used hundreds and hundreds of times in church contexts. The more I heard the words "share the gospel," the more those words started to paint a picture inside me. *What does it mean to "share" something?* I thought. The picture that formed looked something like this:

The gospel is like a chocolate cake—a rich and wonderful chocolate cake. Some people have the chocolate cake, and others do not. If you have cake, if you are one of the lucky ones, you have an important responsibility to "share" your chocolate cake with others.

"Oh boy, oh boy, Tony, you are so lucky to be one of the people with chocolate cake, but don't keep your chocolate cake all to yourself. As you go out into the world, don't forget to share the chocolate cake with all the people who don't have any. Think of those poor people with no cake. Everybody likes cake . . . at least they should. Tony, you own the cake. Others need you to share if they are going to have cake too."

There are some things about this picture that are commendable. But like any picture, it has real limitations. Is there another way to "share"?

During my time at Reed, another picture started to rise inside me. I don't know where it came from or where it found the strength to replace the chocolate cake picture, but it went like this: What if "sharing the gospel" was not so much like sharing a chocolate cake, where one person has privileged access and the other has not? What if sharing the gospel was instead like sharing a sunset?

Sharing a sunset is quite different from sharing cake. Imagine two people standing on a cliff above the Pacific Ocean, watching the sun slowly dip below the horizon. As you share a sunset, you must stand shoulder to shoulder, not face-to-face. When you share a sunset, both observers are caught up in the glory and beauty and mystery. When you share a sunset, everyone present has equal opportunity to contribute; anyone can have a thought to share or implication to suggest. It is a remarkably shared experience.

Now, does this mean that everyone present equally understands all aspects of sunsets? Usually not. For instance, one of the people may have dedicated years of his life to better understanding the nature of photophysics, atmospheric density, and the interrelationship of celestial bodies. All these things can significantly inform the sunset conversation. Sometimes it is fun to understand the science behind why a sunset works the way it does. However, the other person may have different insights to offer to the conversation. Maybe the other person is a watercolor painter and can describe the nature of beauty and its relationship to hope. The conversation can take many turns; these sharing friends, these neighbors may even need to discuss their sadness, because storms have hidden the beauty from their eyes. Being together in their blessing and pain, there are even times when silence may be the best way to "share."

Ultimately, no one can claim to own the sunset. It inspires humility. It releases awe. I can never get enough sunset. I am always left wanting more. A sunset is clearly not painted, created, or contained by humans. It is the work of God. It is a gift to the world. It is something to be shared.

> They who dwell in the ends of the earth stand in awe of
>   Your signs;
> You make the dawn and the sunset shout for joy.

SUNDOWN

Most of what you have read in these Reed chapters all happened during that first year on campus. In total, I walked the Reed garden for almost three years. Over that time many "outsiders" like me would come and journey with our little community for a season, and then they would move on. Some of those friends were like my writer friend, Don. In his time with us, the community inspired his writing and nourished his faith. Other friends were like Kym. She struggled with our admittedly unusual faith culture. For Kym and others, it was too scandalous to bear.

When I first came to campus, I came at the invitation of Saint Michael. When he asked me to stay in his place, he took a real risk. You see, Saint Michael was a part of a larger Christian tribe.

NEIGHBORS AND WISE MEN

I, however, was not a member of his tribe, and that caused some challenges. For the first year or so, the confusion was minimal, and for the most part, our loose partnership functioned without incident. In the months to follow, complications bubbled below the surface.

In the spring of my third year, I was invited by a regional leader to meet for a cup of coffee. James is an accomplished and beloved Christian leader. I was quite honored that he would call and want to spend some time together.

We met at a kitschy coffee shop on Portland's outer east side. The drive took me forty minutes. I found James sitting under the stuffed animal display at the near end of the suburban coffee bar.

At first, our conversation was light. We had met maybe three times over the years, and that allowed for enjoyable banter.

Twenty minutes into our conversation, the atmosphere changed. James's voice and stature stayed the same, but there was a change all the same. You know that moment when you are sitting with your sweetheart and suddenly you realize, "Oh no! This is a breakup conversation"? It is an eerie power of the human subconscious, but somehow we always know. The last time I felt this same sensation in my soul was during my last months in Eastern Europe. Now, as sure as I was breathing, I was feeling it again.

James eased into the breakup dialogue. His words sounded strangely practiced. My head started to swim.

"Tony, you need to know that all of us are really thankful for the years you have put in at Reed; seriously, you have been a real trooper."

"Okaaaaay." Inside I just kept telling myself to stay calm and hear him out. I thought, *Tony, for once in your life, don't overreact!*

James continued. "I really want us to treat this conversation today like a celebration, a celebration of the fact that, well . . . in spite of circumstances, the Lord has shown up all the same."

What does that mean?

"Tony, you know that we have had people at Reed for many, many years now—decades, really. Because of that, we believe it is our responsibility to make sure that the ministry on campus continues in a way that is . . . healthy, that is best for the students. And because of that, to put it simply, we believe the ministry needs to go in a new direction . . . and in order to do that, we need you to step away."

I was turned inside out. "Where is this coming from?" Something had gone terribly wrong. I wanted him to understand. I tried to explain the beauty of our fellowship. He was patient and considerate, but unmoved.

Our conversation lasted another thirty minutes.

His request was obviously not easy for me to accept. It required that we continue talking over the next few weeks. Both of us pleaded our cases. It would be impossible for me to represent both sides accurately; so I will not even try. In the end a line was drawn in the sand. I surrendered. As a result, I walked away and didn't return to Reed for many years.

I tell you this admittedly awkward story for a couple of very important reasons. These reasons are so important that I felt I couldn't leave this Reed season without confessing them to you, even though I know, looking back, I made a number of foolish mistakes.

First, there was my pathology of rejection.

The specter of my departure from Eastern Europe (fueled by my faith failure) swept into my heart the moment James began to "break up" with me. It swept in with such force that it knocked me off balance and stole my ability to think clearly. It pinned me to the ropes. It took my breath.

Let me see if I can explain.

Around the same time as my conversations with James, Aimee and I adopted our first dog. It was a significant life step. (What can

I say? We are dog people.) We found Simon Peter at a private dog shelter not far from Reed College.

He was mangy. The shelter had found him malnourished, abandoned in a crate, and left for dead in an empty parking lot. He had been abused.

Simon is a black mastiff mix, with a head the size of a basketball and a jaw that was engineered to crush bone. When we first met him, he was withered down to a mere eighty pounds and was as skittish as a bird. Because of his past experiences, for years he would flinch anytime someone made a sudden move near him. If I carried a tool through the house or picked up a utensil in the kitchen, he would cower. That is the way the soul works. Even though there was nothing to fear and even though he was strong enough to kill me without breaking a sweat, his previous experiences had rewritten his instincts. He no longer acted rationally.

I reacted the same way to James. And like an animal, I cowered and ran.

In the years that followed, I have thought a lot about my pathology of rejection. I realized that it directed my final decisions at Reed. The more I meditated, the more I realized that its impact runs much, much deeper. It affects decisions I make *every day*.

My pathology of rejection causes me to want to surround myself only with people who feel "safe." It causes me to cower from those I can't predict. It makes me run to the safety of clearly defined hierarchical relationships. It causes me to fear anyone who is different from me, anyone who thinks or believes differently than I do.

I want to protect myself. So, I avoid those who are other.

Avoiding is just preemptive surrender. It separates people. It limits life.

My second confession to you is even more important. In my exit, I betrayed the Reed community; I betrayed my friends.

Through these pages, you have read the significant lessons I was taught by the students at Reed. I am here to tell you, these sorts of lessons are not easy to believe and even harder to live out. After all those experiences, I was still stuck in systems of power, control, and institutional hierarchy. They were so deeply embedded in my soul that even now, years later, my words subtly betray those addictions.

I wanted to change. I had promised the students in a thousand ways that I would fight to treat them as peers. I promised that I would submit to their leadership as we all strove to submit to one another. I promised that I would not make arbitrary decisions without them, especially decisions that would affect our community.

To my shame, when the moment of my personal crisis came, I blocked them out. Never once did I seek their input or submit to their council. Worse, when they came to my aid, to comfort, support, and understand, I stiff-armed my friends because of my rewritten instincts. I gave authority to "outsiders" and not to the ones I had ached and dreamed and believed with. Why? Because in the end it was just too hard. In the end, my faith was weak.

I broke the promise I made to Jared at Nicholas Lebanese restaurant. I broke the promise I made to Mitch that I would not treat him as "just a kid." I broke the promise I made to Nadine, when I insisted her wisdom was essential to us. I broke my promise to Carlos when I told him that even though we believed differently, I would authentically share my spiritual life with him, whatever the cost.

I write these words with fierce intention. I know that the ideas written in these pages are difficult. I know that many of you, like me, will struggle to apply them to your lives, neighborhoods, and spiritual journeys. I write them because the gospel is found through and among these lessons.

Nothing worth doing is ever easy. My failure is evidence of that hope.

Abruptly, my time at Reed came to an end.

Like Adam left Eden, I left Reed. I left it never to return. As

I left, I did not act on the lessons the students had taught me. However, as the months and years pass, I pray that I would find the strength to honor my Reed friends and the lessons they had so graciously given me.

I still thank Jesus for all the ways he spoke to me through their lives and words. I thank him for that chance to walk with him in the tree-filled garden known as Reed College.

The experiences from Reed still grow inside me, and thankfully, it was not the last garden in which God would invite me to walk with him.

SECTION FOUR

COMING HOME

20

NEIGHBOR

"LOCAL IS EVERYTHING! LOCAL IS EVERYTHING!!" GARRETT WAS practically spitting as he spoke.

It was nine o'clock on a Wednesday morning. I had just left Aimee after the boys had been bundled up and scooted off to school. This was a catch-up breakfast. Garrett and I hadn't seen each other in quite some time. We had bumped into each other the week before, and he'd insisted we find a time to talk. We decided on a late breakfast at Muddy's in the Mississippi district of north Portland. The café was only about ten blocks from my house.

Garrett was in rare form for a Wednesday morning. He was dressed all in green, a hand-knit scarf was tugged tightly around his neck, and he wore fingerless gloves.

He was already revved up.

"Man, I am telling you, local is everything. It is way more important than organic." He made air quotes with his fingers as he said *organic*. "It is way more important than sustainable. Any company can claim that something is sustainable, but how do we know? How can we possibly know? Really! Think about it. Where is the accountability? Where is the transparency?"

This was a little much for me. I hadn't even had my coffee yet. I wanted to call a time-out, but it was hopeless. Garrett could not be stopped, and I loved that about him. I just chose to nod along with the rhythm of his diatribe and pray that the server would come soon . . . with lots and lots of coffee.

"Seriously, think about it. A company tells you that their product is sustainable. But what does that really mean? Maybe they *only* shipped it in a recycled box and then slapped a 'sustainable' sticker on it. All the while it was grown with copious amounts of petroleum-based fertilizer and pesticides, not to mention being picked by twenty-first-century slaves on the hillside of some godforsaken province across the world. How do you know?" He cupped his hands in front of his chest as if he were delicately holding the essence of all life.

I needed to show him that I was connecting. "I don't know. How can we know? What would you say?"

"That is just my point, my brother: you can't know. That is why local can span the gulf. It can level the informational playing field. Take this restaurant here, for instance." He started pointing around the café, located on the main floor of a hundred-year-old house right in the heart of the north Portland business district. The surrounding area was full of small boutiques, locally owned restaurants, and nonprofits. "Just look at this place. Look at this locally made art on the walls. Look at the local brew on tap. How 'bout these menus . . ." He picked up a laminated menu and flapped it around in the air. "This is not corporate; this is not the product of some Madison Avenue think tank. This was made by a neighbor. Who do you think owns this place?"

"What?" I wasn't sure if he wanted me to answer or just nod along.

"Who do you think owns this place?!" Garrett was emphatic.

I was a little shocked after such a strong dose of Garrett. So, I collected myself and calmly said, "Well . . . Dyer owns it."

Suddenly, Garrett was speechless. I couldn't believe it. He didn't know what to say. He stammered, "What? I mean . . . I was being rhetorical. You actually know his name?"

"Actually, her name," I said. "Dyer is a woman. She lives around the corner from my house, in the gray house. She has two dogs and a baby boy . . . I believe it is a boy. Anyway, she goes for walks by my house. We say hi."

"Now, *that* is what I am freaking talking about!" Garrett all but screamed. I thought he was going to fly right out of his chair. "That is it. That's it. Man, you know the owner's name! I love that. I love it! Now, follow me on this one . . ." He leaned forward. His brow furrowed. "That is accountability. If you have any questions, you can just go and ask . . . um . . ."

"Dyer."

"Yes, Dyer! You can ask her. Where does she get her coffee beans? What are her recycling habits? Where does she buy her chocolate, her sugar, her . . . pancake batter? Whatever. There is actually someone you can ask." He paused to collect his next thought. "Now, check this out . . . in the twenty minutes since you and I have been sitting here, I watched that blond guy over there lock his bike up out front, enter the door, and go back to the kitchen. He washed his hands and put on an apron. Do you know what that means?"

"I am sure you are going to tell me." I had a playful smirk on my face.

"Local! It means local. He biked here. When you and I pay our bills and leave our tips, we know where it is going. It is going to the blond bike guy, and it is going to Dyer and her son and her two dogs. That is so amazing. It is amazing to be that connected to our money and our world."

I love Garrett. He has a passion for life and a natural revolutionary spirit. When we first met, years before, I told him, "You are an activist looking for a cause." At that we both laughed out loud. The words proved to be prophetic. Over the years since, he had found a life full of causes, and he lives out what he preaches.

"Okay, Garrett. Let me play a little devil's advocate. You and I could have met at a national chain restaurant for breakfast, and it is still full of local people: local servers, local busboys, and local cooks. I mean, it is nice that I know Dyer's name and all, but either way our dollars are going to somebody."

This seemed to wonderfully agitate Garrett. "Great question, great question." He took a moment to straighten the silverware in front of him; then he shot his hands up in front of him, held apart, like opposite ends of a measuring stick. "At a chain restaurant, there is certainly a portion of our dollars that are going to locally employed folks. But the devil is in the details. What *portion* of your money is staying with your neighbors? What portion? And the portion that doesn't go to wages, electricity, and food supplies (probably shipped here from some warehouse in the Midwest, and purchased from God knows where), whatever is left over, where does *that* go?"

"I don't know."

"That's the point. You can't know. But you still have to ask yourself, where is my money going? Is it being siphoned away to the ultrarich or into the hands of people who may really need it . . . people like Dyer?"

Part of me wanted to cool the conversation down a bit. "Garrett, I love your passion, and at the end of the day, your thoughts are really interesting. But it is not exactly a moral issue where I spend every penny. It is the difference between good and great, right? Don't get me wrong; I want to be a supporter of great . . ." I let out a long exhale. "Sometimes good takes a lot less work."

A tinge of disappointment crept into Garrett's eyes, but he was undeterred. "Tony, let me tell you a little story. Is it okay if I tell you a story?" He did not wait for me to answer. He started to organize the various items on the table in front of him—saltshaker, napkin dispenser, and so forth—like a child setting up a scene. "Let's say you own a house on a dozen acres." He placed the dispenser in the middle of the table. "It is not an opulent house. It is reasonable for you and your family. How many kids do you have again?"

"Three boys."

"Okay, the house is reasonable, by Western standards at least, which means it is a palace by global standards, but let's not complicate the conversation."

"Yeah, we wouldn't want to 'complicate' things."

Garrett rolled his eyes. "So, anyway, you have this house. Now, because you love your kids and all your kids' friends, you decide that you want to build a swimming pool. Let's say that you design it yourself and build it the most sustainable way possible. It is a beautiful gift to your family and friends. Now, because you hate chemicals, you come up with a brilliant idea. You decide to redirect the stream that flows through your property to flow into the new pool, providing it with an ever-bubbling source of lovely, pure water." He lined up silverware across the table to represent a stream. "Can you picture it? It is lovely, isn't it? Now, think about your lovely pool . . . Is it an immoral project?"

"Okay, I will play along," I mused. "Let's assume my motives are pure, and since motives are everything, it doesn't seem immoral to me, but I have a feeling you are going to tell me different."

"The devil is in the details. It all depends. It depends—and try to follow me on this one—it all depends on how many questions you are willing to ask." He was on a real roll now. "The part of the story I have not told you is this: a little research shows that the stream, the one you redirected to your swimming pool, used to flow down into the valley, where there are a couple of dozen families that rely on that water to feed their simple crops. Without the water, they have lost their livelihood. Do you see what I am saying?"

I knew that Garrett's story was just a parable, but the applications to real life were starting to make me uncomfortable.

He was not done. "The pool was not necessarily immoral. The desire for fresh water was not immoral. It is when you dig deeper that you discover the implications of your seemingly 'moral' actions. Motivation is not just about the questions you ask; it is also about the questions you don't ask. Ignorance is not bliss. Ignorance is potential destruction. (We vote with our dollars.) Yes, in this story, you voted for a swimming pool, but you also voted to hurt other people."

Garrett grabbed both sides of our small antique table in his hands. He leaned toward me. "Man, I know I have been dominating the conversation. Forgive me for that. But this stuff is important. There is a reason why all the major religious texts spend so much time talking about money. Those ancient dudes were brilliant. They knew that it is not just about being rich or being poor, not entirely. Money is a language. It is a language of morality. And like with so many of the most important issues, morality is found in how deep we are willing to dig. And are we willing to discover . . . and face the implications of our actions?"

Conversations like the one with Garrett that morning at Muddy's are fairly typical in my neighborhood. I am learning to treasure these encounters. I am praying that God will increasingly open my life to my neighbors. I'm beginning to believe that it is imperative that I do so.

(To listen is to love.)

If we love someone, we want to learn the best of who that individual is.

A person's stories and beliefs are the very fabric of his or her identity. To love is to be fascinated by someone's memories, his or her opinions and hopes.

In addition to loving my individual neighbors, I also want to love my neighborhood as a place, the place where God has planted me. Every one of my neighbors is an expert in our shared locality. Each one lives, studies, watches, interprets, listens, and contributes to the DNA of our particular precious place in the world. If I am going to know how to love my place well, I need to harvest the intelligence of everyone: rich and poor, young and old, conservative and liberal, every culture and every background. They are the textbooks and we are the activists.

Finally, and most important, my neighbors transform me. So much so that I no longer believe I can be spiritually whole without them.

My conversation with Garrett was a festival of socioeconomic values. I knew immediately that there were implications of his words that I simply could not yet see. However, while I was walking back home from Muddy's that day, I could not deny his insights.

Garrett spoke about money as a language. He taught me that I vote with every dollar I spend. His words have had an impact on me in very specific and practical ways. Because of his words, I now have a mental trigger every time I open my wallet. In what ways am I voting for goodness and in what ways am I voting for evil? Am I defending my neighbor, the one down the street as well as on the other side of the world? Am I an agent of blessing or harm?

Garrett spoke about money and morality, and he activated it beyond charity or the Sunday morning offering plate. He applied it beyond just family or religious tribe. He applied it to neighbors, whether he knew their names or not. And it staggers me to say he was right. Jesus also talked about money and the poor. He talked about it more than most other topics. He challenged a rich man. He critiqued the motives of giving. He compared the rich to the poor. He evaluated how much a poor widow gave. He spoke on the very nature of the denarius (a coin). For Jesus, financial choices were extremely important. To him, they were foundational to being human. The whole of the Bible supports Jesus' stance with hundreds and hundreds of verses about money. And yet, I have never heard a pastor apply a spirituality of money to the extent that Garrett did. Nor has one changed the way I live like the Garretts in my life.

Finally, Garrett talked about accountability, a term I had only ever really heard in church. And yet it was essential to Garrett. He was fighting for a world of honest exchange. He believed in a world where we are not afraid of each other, a world where we welcome one another into deeper interaction. He wanted to share his thoughts and give others the chance to correct and critique him. He also desperately wanted to be able to ask questions, and to do so in ways that society does not normally condone.

Free and provocative interaction ensures that none of us continues in ignorance.

Open-source confrontation leads to a fuller understanding of morality and can lead to integrated communities of virtue.

21

NAZARETH

"LOCAL IS EVERYTHING." GARRETT'S WORDS STILL ECHO IN MY HEAD. In the years following Reed, life became downright provincial.

Aimee and I got a house in north Portland, just across the river from the Pearl District. We spent our time raising our kids and loving our small house church of faith-friends. We worried about the sorts of things that our neighbors worried about: How do we live without health insurance? How can we support our kids' school in a failing school system? How do we deal with stress? How can we find meaning in the redundancies of life? How can we be spiritually whole?

It was around this time that I was first introduced to the term *spiritual formation*. It was not a new term; it was just new to me. One of the reasons people are drawn to new religions or to new theologies is because they release their imaginations. A new set of terms or fresh patterns helps us break from our ruts; it helps us think in new ways. The idea of spiritual formation was like that for me.

The Bible is full of the most delightful organic questions to describe the path of spiritual formation. Where will you find your spiritual food? What is the source of living water? Where is your spiritual home? Who are your spiritual people? What does it mean to spiritually reproduce? What is your unique role in the spiritual ecosystem? These questions are eternal questions.

These questions supply the "what" of spiritual formation, but it is in the answers that we find life. Let me explain what I mean.

Every animal on earth must answer the same questions listed above, adapted to their physical life, in order to thrive: Where do I find food? What is the source of water? What makes a suitable home? What symbiotic relationships support life? How do I procreate? What is my place in the ecosystem? All these questions define life for any creature. However, the bird will answer these questions very differently than the fish. The questions are identical, but the geography defines the answers. Answers in the rain forest look nothing like the answers in the desert. Answers inside the river look very different from the answers in the Arctic or in Central Park.

It is the same with our spiritual life.

The more my family and community thought about it, the more we knew we needed to understand and love our neighborhood. We needed to draw from this new spiritual ecosystem. Love it for what it is, so we could learn from it. Since I was a boy in Sunday school, I knew the questions. Now we needed to find new answers in our unique and beautiful neighborhood in north Portland.

━━━━━

Jesus grew up in a non-Christian neighborhood. Seriously. There was not one Christian anywhere near his home. In fact, there wasn't a Christian anywhere on the planet.

Sure, he was surrounded by a fair share of Jewish folks. Many of them were probably devout, like his mom. Most of them were probably passive and dismissive about their faith, just like in every community in every culture across the history of the world. That is how it goes with religion.

Looking over Jesus' story, it appears he also regularly encountered Samaritans, pagans, and more than his share of religious hypocrites and power mongers. That was his world.

It seems foolish to even write these words, but when I think about Jesus growing up in Nazareth, it is clear that he had an abiding and dependent relationship with God, his Father. He talked to God. He listened to God. He relied on God—at least from his early teens, and probably long before that.

He also relied on his neighborhood. The neighborhood taught him how to play and how to survive. The neighborhood taught him how to tell a joke, how to pick a fight, and how to win an argument. The neighborhood taught him the street smarts to go along with his Torah smarts. It was the neighborhood that taught him the sort of commoner speech that made the Sermon on the Mount the most influential sermon of all time. He spent his years surrounded by commerce, education systems, entertainment, military, businesses, taxes, and local, regional, and imperial politics. All these things were integrated into his spiritual life.

Jesus was also a carpenter. I have known this since I was old enough to control my bladder. He learned the trade from his father, Joseph. It was the way he supported his family until his public life took off around age thirty. Thirty years is a long time to swing a hammer.

Now, here is a funny question: Why did Jesus never talk about carpentry? There are a lot of red letters in my Bible. Looking over those red letters, there is virtually nothing about carpentry. Doesn't that seem odd? Look at his parables: Why isn't there even one about woodworking? It would seem that carpentry, especially if someone had given thousands of hours of his life to the trade, would provide an unending list of metaphors to build parables around. There are none about shaping wood, fitting joints together, or carefully cutting (even my dad taught me "measure twice; cut once"). There is no parable of the Good Carpenter, no story of the lost hammer or the tool of great price. Not one.

There is, however, a parable about a man who owns a vineyard and lends it out to hired hands. There is a parable about a physician. There are parables about commerce, wage earning, and tax gathering. There are parables about shepherding, husbandry, and numerous aspects of farming. There are parables about fishing, baking, and hosting a celebration. There are parables about sewing, winemaking, and building design (which is the closest Jesus gets to my understanding of carpentry).

This is striking to me.

Where did Jesus learn about all these things? It was not a passive knowledge either. He had learned about these topics so well that he could deftly and effortlessly apply them to the most profound aspects of life. He could spontaneously discuss them with thousands of eyes on him or during a hostile interrogation.

Where did he learn them? He must have learned these things from his neighbors. Where else? Jesus did not grow up in a mountain monastery or in a palace. He lived in a real town, surrounded by real people. He was affected, influenced, and transformed by the experts all around him. He learned about these things from hanging with the folks in the house across the street, from skipping alongside travelers and while loitering with other kids in the city square. He was integrated with them and they with him. He was incarnated in his very particular time and place.

The parables are a wonderful window into Jesus' spiritual formation.

Jesus grew up in first-century Nazareth, a village in ancient Israel maybe a day's walk from Jerusalem. I have never been there. I don't own a time machine. I do get to see it, though. I get to see it through the words and life of Jesus.

Jesus was spiritually formed in Nazareth. And now, each of us needs to consider the particular location of our unique formation.

We, my family and community, are growing up in inner north Portland. This is our village.

Our neighborhood is full of coffee shops, microbreweries, and food carts. We have a light-rail train. We have a school system that is struggling to survive. We have young, hip communities side by side with long-established communities. We have new wealth and old poverty. We have one of Portland's original red-light districts. We have a palatial cliff-top private university. We have a few churches, but most sit nearly empty on Sundays. We have people.

The people make the parish. They are our neighbors.

As we walk through our place, we are trying to follow Jesus' lead. As near as we can tell, that is the best summary of what Jesus asked of us: "Follow me." So that is what we are trying to do. In following his lead, within our neighborhood, we are being spiritually formed.

Two thousand years ago, Jesus wrote parables from his interactions with his neighbors. Today, as we walk with him, Jesus continues his habit of parable writing. Only now it's not Nazareth, this neighborhood is different. He is writing new parables through our spiritually forming neighbors all around.

In every place, Jesus has parables to share, if only we have ears to hear. Here are some of the parables from our neighborhood. Ask yourself, what are the fresh stories of formation from your place and time?

22

THE GOOD SAMARITAN

I MET ROBBIE IN A PARK. HE WANDERED RIGHT UP TO ME.

I remember the moment. He was handsome. He was cautious.

I remember that Amber and Noel were playing with a volleyball. I remember that Bryan was tending the barbecue. There was laughter coming from the picnic table. And in walked Robbie.

I asked him if he wanted to join us. He said that was why he had come.

Robbie grabbed his gear and entered our lives forever.

Robbie was a traveler. He had traveled a long road from Southern California to Eugene, Oregon, and had only just arrived in Portland.

Along the way he had found a wife. Then he lost her.

He was still in his early twenties, but there was already so much sorrow there. This was one of the very first things he shared with us about his story.

We became close very quickly. I treasure that.

From our first days together, we talked often about things of the spirit. Robbie's spiritual travels had him at a crossroads. He told us about his upbringing. His parents had been long divorced.

His father was an influential evangelical minister, kind and wise. His mother was now more "new age," and very content in her spiritual life.

Part of the reason Robbie joined our lives was because we were Jesus folk. He was looking for some people to process faith with, and so that mysterious compass that guides our lives led us straight to each other.

It was beautiful and honest to watch him process his faith with us over those first years together. He taught me so much.

In the end Robbie just couldn't accept Christianity, try as he might. I remember the conversation as we sat at our small kitchen table.

"If all the people of the world consumed at the rate that Americans consume, did you know that it would take five and a half earths just to support us all?" Robbie was not ranting. He was sober and careful with his words. That was his way.

Back in those days, we were living in a little ranch-style home. It was little more than a front room with small bedrooms attached on either side. The front room had a wall with curved edges and outdated electrical outlets. We painted the wall red. From where we sat at our little table, we could look out the wide front window at the busy street. There was a dilapidated lot across the street, full of rusted-out cars.

I answered, "You're saying that if all six billion people in the world ate like Americans, drove like Americans, and shopped like Americans, it would take five and a half earths to support our"—I tried to find the right words—"addiction to consumption?"

"That is what the data shows."

"I didn't know that, but it doesn't surprise me."

Robbie continued. "Our world is massively overtaxed. Yet we continue on as if everything is okay. We keep living without acknowledging that we are on a path of self-created destruction.

The population is not decreasing. Our consumption is not decreasing. Our greed is not decreasing."

Believe it or not, these words surfaced during a conversation about faith. In many ways this juxtaposition of God and earth was new to me. It was not new to Robbie. Earth and God were necessarily intertwined. I had not been raised to see the connection so strongly. Robbie was helping me with that.

"We never talked about this sort of thing in church growing up," I said. "In fact, we made fun of hippies and tree-huggers. For the most part I was taught that they were missing the point. Of course, no one claimed that a good Christian wants to destroy the environment. But earth care was a distant secondary issue at best."

Robbie had sorrow in his eyes. "Yes. That is exactly what I am talking about. At the end of the day, the Christian church has no coherent answer for earth care. And for that reason I now know I could *never* be a Christian."

Before this, he had always been exploratory in his language. This was different. He said it like the strike of a gavel. This was not the only evidence to his rejection of the Christian faith, but it was his closing argument. At this, his flirtations with Christianity were officially over. And, he has not looked back since.

Despite our metaphysical differences, Robbie was family. He lived with us off and on over the years. My boys call him "Jahjee," which comes from an Albanian word for uncle. He is their favorite.

In time, the travel bug nibbled enough of Robbie's soul that he could stand it no longer. He came by the house and announced that he was packing up a single backpack and his touring bike and moving to New Zealand. He told us that he only had a few hundred dollars in his pocket, but he didn't care. He would work organic farms on his way to seeing every beautiful inch of the islands.

And just like that, he was gone.

197

He would write. We would try to follow his adventures. Robbie was happy. He was inspired.

After many months his soul scrapbook was full to overflowing with the sights, sounds, and smells of New Zealand. So, he bundled up his few belongings and moved to Thailand. There he found a great job. It paid well. He was good at it. And most of all, it was the sort of job that would open a door to the world. Like a character in a fairy tale, Robbie would get to fulfill his dreams. The world was literally laid before him as a gift, and he would be paid to experience it.

Then Robbie's grandfather fell ill. Unexpectedly, Robbie flew back to the States for a short visit. During his stay he managed to find time to come to Portland to visit his family here: his mom, his sister, and us.

When he arrived, he found us in one of our most difficult seasons. We knew he could only visit a couple of days, so Aimee and I tried to put on a happy front. But when you really know someone, the "happy front" game never really works. He saw right through it and tenderly asked the right questions to get to the truth.

The struggles were becoming crises. My business was failing. I was working long hours and yet, for several months now, had brought home little to no income. We were flat broke. Our house was at risk. Our bank account was at zero, and our reserves had dried up long before. I was stressed. Aimee was exhausted. We had three small boys, two of which were still in diapers. And our marriage was in critical condition.

Like a geyser, we blurted out the hurts and needs we had been holding in for so long. Robbie listened. His eyes were kind and his spirit was open. He just kept saying that he hadn't realized. We told him that we weren't hiding it from him. We just hadn't known how to explain all this when he lived so far away. He nodded with understanding.

Robbie's last night in town, he came over for dinner. He helped put the boys to bed, as was his custom, and the three of us sat down to eat.

As she always did, Aimee had made the best of what little we had, and there was a small feast waiting in the dining room.

Robbie came in the room and said to Aimee, "You shouldn't have—"

Before he could finish, she walked over and gave him a hug and said, "We have a theology of celebration. Tonight we are celebrating you, and in whatever way we can, the meal needs to reflect that celebration."

We did celebrate. We shared a cheap bottle of wine. We put our cares to the side. We told old stories. We laughed like we hadn't laughed in a long time. And for a moment, we pressed pause on life. And like the Sabbath of old, we rested together.

When dinner came to an end, Robbie placed his silverware in the middle of his plate and wiped his mouth with his napkin. He made a moaning sound as if to say he could not eat another bite. "Thank you so much for dinner."

Our eyes drifted around the dining room for a few moments, looking at nothing in particular, a peaceful pause at the end of a pleasant meal.

Then Robbie spoke. He sat up tall in his chair. His words were deliberate. "There is something that we need to talk about."

It was not like him to be so directive in his tone. He had my attention.

"Before I say anything, you guys need to understand something. What I am about to say is not open to discussion. You guys don't get a vote in my life on this one. There will be no argument. No discussion. Do you understand?"

Aimee and I looked at each other. Our eyebrows were raised.

We shrugged at each other and told Robbie, "Okay, we agree. Now, what have you done?"

He smiled at this. But he quickly put his smile away. He would not be deterred. "It is my humble opinion that you guys need some help. And I, for better or worse, am going to give it to you. Here's the deal." He hesitated for effect. "I'm moving in."

"What?!"

"Ah, ah, ah . . . no discussion. Remember?"

Robbie was not messing around. Over the next ten minutes, he explained all of his reasoning. "I am moving in. Aimee, I am going to help with the boys and give you some time away. I am also going to help with the bills. You two are going to go out on dates again. I am going to get a part-time job so I can still be available." He went on to explain that he would also be looking into graduate school. This was not a flippant decision. He committed, "I will stay with you as long as it takes."

We couldn't obey his "no discussion" rule. We asked him about his job. He told us he had already called and quit. We asked him about his dreams of travel and adventure. Since the first time we met him, he had confided in us his desire to wander the world. We could not sit by and let him give all that up.

Robbie spoke carefully, making clear eye contact with Aimee and then with me. "I have been thinking a lot these last two days . . . about who I am and what I care about most. I love my job, and God knows I love to travel, and I will never lose my desire to see the world. But at the end of the day, the most important things in my life are my family. You guys are my family. And if I can't put my life on hold for you, then what kind of person would I be? So, it's settled. No more discussion."

And with that, he placed his palms down on the edge of the table and pushed himself up. He stacked our three plates one on top of the other and collected the silverware. As he walked into the kitchen, he declared over his shoulder, "I'll do the dishes."

———

In the story of the good Samaritan, a traveler inconveniences his life for another. He is a foreigner, and his spiritual heritage is a significant part of the scandal of the story. The good Samaritan stops his life for someone else. He gives his time, his resources, his money, his reputation, and his future plans. Just like Robbie.

As a boy, I was taught that the parable was about loving someone who is different from you, and that is certainly part of the message. However, I don't remember anyone going out of his way to point out that the spiritual hero, the gospel example in the story, was a religious foreigner. The Samaritan and the wounded Jew were at religious odds, and yet the Samaritan gave and gave up.

Generosity is undoubtedly a virtue. It flows from the character of God, who gives and sacrifices for us. However, if I honestly reflect on the lessons I have been subtly taught over my life, there are important limitations on generosity. I was taught that wisdom and temperance demand limitation. We are to be generous with our money, to a point. Generosity means 10 percent, and if you have the gift of generosity, it might mean 20. We are to be generous with our time. That means Sundays, two weekday evenings, and maybe a week in the summer. We are to be generous with our plans and dreams . . . but what does that really mean?

For Robbie, generosity meant 100 percent. Generosity meant all his time. Generosity included giving up his plans and dreams. Love is the only constant.

Love thy neighbor as thyself.

And the man asked Jesus, "Who is my neighbor?"

Generosity is not defined by what we can afford. It is defined by what we cannot afford.

Because of what my family has been taught by Robbie and others like him, we have tried to change the culture of our home. We have tried to live with open doors. We have tried to hold lightly to our money and things. We are praying that God would help us be good neighbors.

23

PARABLES

THERE IS AN INTERESTING PHRASE IN THE TRAVEL TEACHINGS OF Jesus. He would encourage his listeners to "look": Look at the birds . . . Look at the fig tree . . . Look at the fields . . . Look at the denarius. It is as if Jesus' eyes were ever open to the revelation of God's kingdom all around him. Not only is Jesus ever open, but he seems to be ever calling anyone who will listen to join him in his expectancy of truth.

THE TREASURE IN A FIELD

On my way home one afternoon, I looked across the street and saw Heather. She was, like so many days before, working in her garden. Heather is unusual, delightfully so. It is typical to catch her with a smudge of dirt on her face or chicken poop stuck to her shoes. You probably know someone like her.

On this particular day Heather was wearing a periwinkle wool sweater with a hole worn through one elbow and knee-high galoshes. She kept shoving the sleeves of her sweater up around her elbows. She had to push them with her wrists because her gloved hands were caked in the most delicious black dirt. Of course, within moments the sleeves would slip right back down and she would need to shove them up again.

I crossed the street and said, "I see your garden has migrated to your front yard," making neighborly conversation.

"Yep. I ripped out most of the lawn on this side of the yard, and the other side may go next spring. We will have to see."

I looked at her remaining grass. It was perfect, a carpet of green. She had no weeds, and the lawn was flat, not all ripply, like the grass at my house. "Your grass looks pretty good to me; why would you want to rip it up?" It was more curiosity than it was an accusation, and she took it as such.

Heather was now on her knees, troweling around in the dirt. "Do you know where the idea of a lawn, particularly a large front lawn, came from?"

"Nope."

"It was a sign of wealth, and some would say a sign of oppression. Originally only the richest of families could afford to have land that was intentionally unproductive. A lawn was a giant billboard declaring to the surrounding peasants: 'We have so much land we can waste it. We are rich and you are poor; deal with it.'"

"Interesting," I said. "I have never heard that before. Is that why you are tearing out your lawn, because you think grass is oppressive?"

Heather laughed. "Of course not. I just think it is an interesting historical note. But symbols do have meaning." She turned over and sat crisscross applesauce in the dirt. She blew air out of the side of her mouth to push away a strand of hair hanging in her face. "I am in the front yard because I don't like to hide away in the backyard. By the way, do you want to hear where the front porch came from?"

I chuckled. "That's okay."

"Suit yourself. Anyway, I live like this because I love plants, and fresh vegetables and fresh eggs."

"Heather, have you ever done the math to see how much all this costs you? Chicken feed and organic fertilizers and materials and tools. This stuff isn't cheap. Are you getting vegetables any cheaper than if you just bought them at the store? And then you wouldn't be stuck out here, covered in dirt all the time." I immediately regretted saying it. Once again I had left my brain filter at home, and I was blabbing without thinking.

Heather, of course, was unfazed. "I don't do all this to save money, though your math may not be as accurate as you think. I do all this to be whole. I believe my soul was designed to be connected to the soil and to other living things. I think one of the reasons that our world is so consumeristic is because we are numb and floating through life. Grocery stores have a purpose, but they also effectively disconnect us from the soil. Soil is land and land is geography. How can a physical being exist disconnected from its physical space? I believe we were made to have geography under our fingernails." At this she slipped off one glove and showed me the black under all five nails.

———

What does it mean to be human? Heather has some strong opinions about that. We were only acquaintances, but I have no reason to suspect that Heather is a Bible reader. From my perspective, at the time, her view of human identity and its connection to the plants and animals seemed a bit—how shall I say this?—out of balance.

I *knew* where human identity comes from. It comes from our relationship with God first. Humanity was created with a special interconnectedness to the divine. God said, "Let us make mankind in our image." I had known this verse since I was a young man. It was found on the first page of my Bible. It was the sort of identity statement that sets the rest of the biblical story in motion.

Soon after my conversation with Heather, I found myself

reading those first pages of my Bible again. Have you ever had that sensation that new verses had been magically inserted into a beloved text? This time felt like that.

At the bottom of the Bible's first page, I came again to those beautiful identity words: God said, "Let us make mankind in our image." It was as inspiring as ever, this idea that our very lives are designed to be intertwined with others and with God.

Then I noticed, maybe for the first time, that this was only the first line of a much longer thought. The paragraph continued. "Then God said, 'I give you every seed-bearing plant on the face of the whole earth and every tree that has fruit with seed in it. They will be yours for food. And to all the beasts of the earth and all the birds in the sky and all the creatures that move along the ground—everything that has the breath of life in it—I give every green plant for food.' And it was so."

Had I always taken the "God's image" verse out of context? Had I missed the greater narrative? Had I in fact missed some aspect of our core identity? After a lifetime of reading my Bible, I was just discovering what Heather instinctually knew.

———

Back at home, Aimee and I began a new conversation about who we are and what we want to be a part of; how we wanted to raise our boys and how we want them to be connected to their world. We knew that some of the answer is found in that identity paragraph from the Bible's first page. The goal was to be more fully relationally connected to both people and planet. There are probably a million ways to do that, but we wanted to reflect the ways of our particular time and space, our neighborhood. Soon, we were ripping out sod and putting in gardens. We did it like Heather, in our front yard, so we could share the experience with our neighbors.

The next spring we got chickens. And that started a whole other adventure.

THE LOST SON

"Do you want to know one of the most gruesome sentences in the English language?" Dillon asked as we shared a beer.

We were sitting at one of the heavy picnic tables in the Amnesia Brewing beer garden. Amnesia is known for its bruising ales. It was a warm afternoon, and about half of the twentyish picnic tables had beer connoisseurs lingering over midday dialogues.

"That sounds ominous," I said in response to Dillon's question. I stretched my mouth wide and made a creepy lizard face.

Dillon picked up his pint glass and held it up in front of him. "The most gruesome sentence in the English language is 'You will never guess how little I paid for this!'" With that, he banged the glass to the table with a thud and a slosh.

I watched little puddles of his beer foam on the rough tabletop. Then I told him, "I am not tracking with you."

Dillon continued. "I am baffled by this American addiction to bragging about how little we pay for things. I understand that some of it comes from a desire for a deal. But sometimes a deal is not a deal at all."

I scowled. "If that was your best attempt to clarify your point, this is going to be a long conversation."

Dillon nodded to himself with a furrowed brow. He could see that I was going to take some work. "Sometimes a deal is not a deal. Okay, let's say you go into one of those big ole you-can-buy-anything-you-can-think-of stores. And let's say you buy a—I don't know—a toaster." Dillon bobbled his head around as he said it; it was clear that he was not fully satisfied by his choice of "toaster." He decided not to let it distract him and continued. "So you go in and buy a toaster, and the toaster costs something like $9.99. You are excited. And your first thought is, *What an amazing price.* Now, here is the question: Why does this price excite you?"

I thought for just a moment. "It is pretty obvious, isn't it?" I was still not on Dillon's frequency. "It excites me because it is cheap."

"And what does 'cheap' *mean?*" Dillon's eyes were wide, and his head cocked slightly to the side, like a spaniel puppy.

I still didn't get it, and he could see the confusion written all over my face.

So he rescued me. "It means that something inside you knows it should cost more. That is what it means. When you think of a toaster, what price comes to mind? Think about it. I think, fifty dollars for a nice one and twenty dollars for an entry-level toaster. Would you agree?"

"I guess." I felt like I was tracking, though I still didn't know exactly what we were talking about.

"Let me cut to the chase." Dillon was ready to make his point. "You know that the toaster should cost twenty dollars, at least, and yet you are getting it for ten. So the question you should ask yourself, the question we somehow never ask ourselves, is 'Where did the other ten dollars go?'"

What?! He might as well have been speaking Vietnamese. "What do you mean, 'Where did the other ten dollars go?'"

He was right. I had never asked myself that totally obvious question. Where *did* the other ten dollars go?

After another long sip from his beer, Dillon continued. "Making a toaster is a pretty static formula. You can measure and predict the whole process: materials, labor, manufacturing, assembly, energy, utilities, transportation, storage, stocking, employees, etc. All these expenses are essential to the process, and each one of these steps has a cost. Most of those costs are fixed. There is almost no wiggle room. Do you follow me so far?"

"I am *really* trying."

Dillon seemed satisfied by my attempt to understand, so he continued. "Okay, fuel costs are set by the market. Utilities costs are set by the market. In America, employees come with a set minimum cost. The space on a ship to transport the toaster to America has a set cost. At the end of the day, most everything has a set cost that must be accounted for in *your* price of $9.99."

It was starting to click for me. "And you are saying that you can't possibly squish all those collected costs into a $9.99 price tag. Am I following you?" Without waiting for an answer, I attempted an explanation. "That means that the store must be swallowing the loss?"

Dillon laughed out loud. "I seriously doubt that." He continued a barely audible chuckle for a few more seconds. "I believe there is a more likely explanation. From my estimation there are only a few places to recoup the kind of costs we are talking about. Only a few costs that companies can really fiddle with. The biggest one is probably labor. That is where they can really cook the numbers." He picked up a peanut out of the bowl on the table and worked the shell between his fingertips.

"Are you sure?" My skepticism showed through.

"On one level, if you need to save a few pennies, you can put your manufacturing in a country with a lower cost of living and still pay people a reasonable wage, by human rights standards. But if you need to save a whole bunch of pennies, sometimes it is easiest to find places where you don't have to pay people at all. Like it or not, there are twenty-seven million slaves in the world today. That is not my number; that is the United Nations' number. And just to take it one step further, many of those slaves are children." At this his eyes went hot. He snatched up a peanut, reeled back his arm, and chucked the nut, shell and all, clear to the other side of the street, where it bounced off the hood of a Volvo. "Crap," he murmured. "I didn't mean to hit the car."

Dillon was not just being a smarty-pants. This stuff really affected him. I watched him in a sullen cloud, grinding peanut shells into the table. I just let the silence float between us. Dillon has a three-year-old boy, and I guessed he was imagining his boy forced into a factory.

After a few moments he spoke again, but this time he didn't look up at me. "Remember that kid that disappeared last year? The kid with the glasses and the toothy grin?"

"The one that they could never find, and everyone suspected the stepmom?" I answered. "Yeah, I remember. He was on the news every night. You can still find fliers posted around the city."

"Well, that is a sad story, no doubt. And I still hope they find that innocent kid. But I can't help but wonder, how can we put all that money toward trying to find this one little Caucasian kid from the suburbs . . . and never even think to worry about millions of lost kids on the other side of the world. Kids who are lost in slavery. And I am horrified to say this, but it is my lust for cheap crap that is helping to fund their living horror show."

Another peanut launched into the air. This one cleared the Volvo.

Jesus said, "It would be better for them to be thrown into the sea with a millstone tied around their neck than to cause one of these little ones to stumble."

THE WISE SERVANT

I have a neighbor named Sam. Sam and I have never spoken more than a simple hello when passing along the street. Sam is not rude; he is busy. Sam is the mayor of Portland.

I like Sam. I don't agree with all of his politics, but I could say the same thing about any public figure. The very fact that he lives in north Portland, as opposed to one of the more protected areas of town, should tell you something.

It can't be easy being a mayor, especially of a city like Portland. Close to a million people all tugging you in different directions. A whole region built on pioneering and activist values. Couple that with high unemployment and a failing economy. He has a near impossible job. For that reason, he has my admiration.

One of Sam's responsibilities is to care for the children of our city, particularly in the realms of schools and social services. I once heard Sam say, "Everybody says that Portland is one of the most livable cities in the world, and it is. But how dare we call ourselves 'livable' when so many of our most innocent are suffering?" I think he is right.

Portland has a failing school system. That is just a fact. The basic resources are not there to provide more than a bare minimum of school services. Every year, more and more teachers are laid off. Classes get bigger and bigger and then meet for fewer and fewer days each year. Any learning beyond reading, writing, and arithmetic has already been amputated from the budget. The schoolyards are full of weeds. The schools rely on parent volunteers to supply office help during the week and tend the grounds on weekends.

This is just the way it is. The burden for all this ultimately falls on the shoulders of government, and I know that Sam feels the weight of that responsibility.

The city budget for Portland is already stretched beyond recognition. Sam wants to help schools, but what can he do? He has no more money. He has no other resources to pull from. It is hard to imagine how he could further downsize.

So where does one go when he runs out of money? Where does one go when she's out of financial options? Well, he does what any of us would do. We call our friends. And if we don't have the sort of friends who will help, we make new friends . . . anywhere we can.

That is exactly what Sam did. He made the most unlikely friends. Sam chose to extend an olive branch to Portland's conservative Christians. I kid you not. Sam is considered by most to be quite liberal in his politics. He also happens to be gay. I think it is fairly safe to say that the gay community and the conservative Christian community have not played together very well over the decades. I am not placing blame; I am just stating what is a fairly undisputed fact. The gay community and the Christian community have been the societal equivalent of the Sharks and the Jets from *West Side Story*. Not pretty.

The conservative Christian community does not support Sam. They did little to help him get elected, and if he were to run again, they would account for a powerful block of votes against him. But for Sam, this time it wasn't about getting elected. It was about helping kids.

Sam met with local Christian leaders and said, "Our schools need funding, resources, and manpower. How can we be friends for the greater good?"

As a result, Sam, as the spokesman for local government, entered a beautiful partnership with some of the most conservative streams of Christianity in our city. Churches were invited into partnerships with local schools and in many cases were offered unprecedented access to the campuses and student populations.

My neighborhood, the area known as north Portland, has many of the city's most failing schools. Not far from our house sits a historically hurting high school. However, thanks to these paradigm-shattering efforts, there are currently dozens of social services that never existed before—all because of this city/church partnership. Funding is flowing in, and coaches and staff are being supplied by generous church congregations.

This is what is possible when we dare to make friends where strangers once stood. This is what is possible in a community of reciprocity. This is what is possible if we can see past protectionism and embrace a belief in abundance.

If only I could have the courage and generosity of spirit to look to those who are not like me. If only I could reject my natural state of suspicion. If only I could embrace the other and be a friend.

24

THE PRODIGAL

"WHAT IF WE JUST TOOK JESUS AT HIS WORD?"

At first it seemed like the most obvious question.

The more we thought about it, the more we realized it was not obvious at all. Also, it was not easy. In fact, it might just change the way we viewed everything.

In the end, we discovered, we would never be the same.

The idea was simple, beautifully simple. It was built on the themes of the Jesus Dojo, a formation exercise conceived by some friends in San Francisco. We called it the Be at Peace Project. The plan: to choose a single teaching of Jesus, one at a time, and figure out how to courageously apply it to our lives.

Bobbin is an intriguing bloke.

He is a badger of a man. I once heard that pound for pound,

the badger is the last creature you would ever want to tangle with. Bobbin has a tenacious spirit, a compact frame, and a never-back-down mentality. In other words: a badger.

Bobbin is a paradox. On the one hand he is meticulous about his appearance. He has well-groomed hair, perfect sideburns, and an always smooth-shaven face. On the other hand, I have almost never seen him in a collared shirt. Graphic T-shirts and jeans are about all he needs. His most striking feature, though, is his many piercings: nose, between his eyes, the back of his neck, and a couple of epic holes in his ears the size of spools (and these are just the beginning of his holey-ness.)

He is antiestablishment, antigovernment, and a conspiracy theorist. Bobbin keeps a flag in his room. It is not there to be flown or saluted. It is there for protest. It is there just in case the occasion demands that he light it on fire. That is Bobbin.

He is opinionated. He is unapologetic.

———

When we started the Be at Peace Project, we threw the invitation out to neighbors and friends. We weren't sure if anyone would show up. Our invitation was "Come learn how to take Jesus at his word." It is an interesting proposition but a bit nebulous, and we imagined we would only speak to a small group of people.

To our delight, about a dozen people came.

Arriving a few minutes late . . . in walked Bobbin. This was a particular surprise.

Now, there was no doubt that Bobbin was a cherished friend. He had long been a participant in our Sunday night community dinner. He was loyal, to be sure. But just a few weeks before, Bobbin had ranted to the table about how he could not deal with Christianity and that he now considered himself more Buddhist than anything.

In spite of all that, here he was. Bobbin joined us to explore the Jesus-way.

He acted like it was the most normal thing in the world that he would come. I had a hard time hiding my grin as he tried to saunter into the living room, pretending like it was no big deal. Have you ever seen a badger saunter? Funny.

It took us several weeks and a comprehensive investigation of the teachings of Jesus to decide on our first experiment. Once again the idea was simple: choose a single teaching of Jesus, and seek a way to courageously apply it.

After much prayer, argument, and laughter, we landed on a teaching that, to tell you the truth, surprised us all. I guess that is how it works with free-flow group discernment, particularly if God's Walk-Alongside Spirit is an active voice in the room.

We landed on, "Therefore, if you are offering your gift at the altar and there remember that your brother or sister has something against you, leave your gift there in front of the altar. First go and be reconciled to them; then come and offer your gift." Like I said, a very surprising passage. Not one we would have naturally picked.

After a delightful dance of wills, we determined to practice radical personal reconciliation with the people in our lives. To accomplish this we chose to interview three people each: friends, family, or coworkers. We would ask them these relationally direct questions: Is there anything unreconciled in our relationship? Is there any way that I have been a poor friend [son, sister, coworker, etc.]? In what ways have I made it hard for you to tell me the truth? In what ways have you felt manipulated by me? In what ways have I hidden my true self from you?

The goal was to listen, to ask for forgiveness, and then to make restitution. The goal was to be at peace with others and then free to approach God, as Jesus had taught.

The more we talked, the hotter the room got. The heat radiated from the corner where Bobbin sat. He was horrified by all of this. He practically hijacked the conversation. "Do we have to do this? What if they won't listen to us? Do we have to ask all the questions? What if they can't stop telling us ways we've screwed up? What if the conversation takes hours? What if we disagree with what they say? Do we have to ask for forgiveness?"

Bobbin was petulant, but he was also saying the things that all of us felt but were afraid to ask. It had been a long process. We had all affirmed every step we had taken along the way; still, none of us were completely sure of where we had ended up. As a group, we reminded Bobbin and ourselves that this sort of humility could be life changing. We reminded ourselves that it was not a quid pro quo. Our plan was about one person listening to the hurts of the other . . . and then begging for forgiveness.

At evening's end, Bobbin was quiet. He sat in the camel-colored chair by the fireplace and stared at those few questions printed on the index card in his hand. I could only imagine what was going through his fiery mind.

———

A week later we reconvened, bearing the stories of our reconciliations. The room was energetic. There was a collective exhale of relief that this week's experiment was over.

We began to tell the tales of our faulting humility and relational recovery. Kris, our furry-faced musician, talked of an old friend who had helped him see how selfish he is. Kathryn, kind and sublime, told about talking to a fellow teacher. Amber had dared to interview her dad.

Around the room we went, each sharing some nugget of personal revelation and the general power of courageous confession. Quietly, Bobbin sat. He barely made eye contact as all the others spoke.

The time came when everyone had shared some story, with one radiating exception: Bobbin. We all knew the week had been particularly difficult for him, and we wanted to give him space to share only if he felt he could.

Finally he spoke. His voice was low and hesitant. "I interviewed six people."

We erupted. "You what!? We were only shooting for three." And truth be told, many of us had only completed one or two.

Bobbin was sheepish. "I know. The truth is, I needed the practice, or maybe I needed to build up my courage."

"What do you mean?" Jeremiah asked. Of anyone in the group, Jeremiah was a model of explorative humility, and the honesty in his eyes was enough to woo Bobbin to continue.

"As soon as we landed on this *stupid* experiment, I knew exactly what I needed to do. I tried to talk myself out of it in a million ways, but I knew. I was supposed to track down my ex-wife and ask her the questions."

Bobbin is a young man, still in his midtwenties, and not everybody in the room even knew he had been married before. Those of us who did also knew they had been estranged since breaking up. The separation had been nasty. The wounds for both were deep. We knew Bobbin was still angry. We could only imagine how strong her emotions still were.

It took us some time to coax the story out of him. He started with his five "warm-up" interviews that were quite dramatic in and of themselves, but it was the exchange with the wife, whom he had once pushed away, that changed us all.

Out of respect for Bobbin, I will not share the details of her words as she answered each of his questions. I will tell you this: the conversation lasted over an hour. Over an hour of unfiltered accusations from unbridled hurts. Bobbin asked the questions, and then to his credit, he shut up. "Is there anything unreconciled in our relationship? In what ways was I a poor husband? In what ways have you felt manipulated by me?" Each answer lasted fifteen minutes or longer. Indictments spewed like acid from a fire hose.

Bobbin confessed again and again how she was right, maybe not every word, but she was right. He knew it. Through each of the questions, he tried to stay emotionally present. He desperately tried to remember every offense.

When she was finally done, having squeezed out every memory like an empty toothpaste tube, Bobbin spoke. He spoke back to her his betrayals, each in his own words, without excuse. Then mustering the remaining dregs of his soul, he begged her to forgive him. Offense after offense, he asked her to please forgive him. He had been wrong. She deserved better.

For a moment they sat. They were little more than deflated balloons.

In the end she looked at him. She was done and wanted Bobbin to know it. She said, "I will *never* forgive you."

———

We sat in my living room mesmerized and heartbroken. Bobbin tried to play if off like it was no big deal. He said, "It is what it is. I am still glad that I did it. It was important for me to apologize."

We tried to get him to talk more about his emotions, but Bobbin, like most of us, keeps these sorts of cards pretty close to the chest.

Finally, he remembered. "By the way, she did text me the next day."

"Really, what did she say?"

"It was pretty short, but she said, 'Thank you.'"

Kris said, "Well, that's something that seems pretty significant."

"Yeah, it was. She also said I had 'set her free.'"

He made no excuses to us about his brokenness. He had made no excuses to her either. We just sat and watched our anarchist-badger friend live out the story of reconciliation right before our eyes.

Bobbin is my hero.

Relationships are like a resort hotel. There is so much potential, so much to share. There are innumerable rooms to explore together, so much grandeur and opportunities for delight. Then we start to get to know the other person. We start to allow others to know us. We give them the ammunition to hurt us. Then we hurt them back. With each piece of pain, with each betrayal, with each abuse of trust, we begin to lock off the hotel. We start with one room at a time. Pretty soon we lock off entire floors, removing them from even the potential of interconnectedness. Most relationships get relegated to only the safest places of exchange, the lobby and maybe the tennis courts. Some relationships eventually sound the death knell and lock the entrance doors forever.

Bobbin refused to leave their relationship locked away. He acted in faith. We have established a culture of abandoning relationships, but Bobbin is antiestablishment. We have created habits of passive retreat, but Bobbin is an activist.

He busted down the door. He busted it with silence, with listening, with humility, with contrition and remorse . . . at least for one conversation. And sometimes one conversation can change your life. Sometimes it will even "set us free." I don't know if Bobbin would admit this, but I believe his courage released even more freedom in him than it did in her.

Truth be told, Bobbin and his ex-love did not exactly throw open the entire hotel of their lost relationship. But they began to stroll around the lobby again. And in time, who knows?

Jesus said, "Salt is good, but if it loses its saltiness, how can you make it salty again? Have salt among yourselves, and *be at peace* with each other." Paul borrowed Jesus' words when he said, "As much as it depends upon you, *be at peace* with all people."

The dream to *be at peace* is an invitation from Jesus. It is a courageous undertaking.

These are just some of the parables that Jesus is writing all around us. They are coming from our neighbors, those people we are living with, listening to, and learning from. These are the streams of transformation that are flowing through our very specific place in the story of God. What streams are flowing through yours?

Closing

EPIPHANY

THERE IS AN ANCIENT CHRISTIAN CELEBRATION THAT IS FOUND ON the church calendar a couple of weeks after Christmas. It is the day of remembrance of the Magi who visited Jesus as a babe. The ancient church saw it necessary to yearly revere the pagan scholars from the East. These "wise men" were not Jews, and they certainly were not Christians, as there were no such things as Christians at this point in history. These men loved and longed for the story of God. Their hearts were turned toward it. They were compelled to follow that story wherever it led. They were ready to give up their time, travels, and wealth in their devotion.

The day the ancient church chose to commemorate the wise men was called *Epiphany*: a word we use today to mean "a profound lesson from a surprising source or circumstance."

As you read these pages, I pray that my faith friends have spoken to you, as they have spoken to me, and that you have had epiphanies of your own.

After reading, you may think that I am not a very good Christian. And you would probably not get much argument from me. I struggle with doubt. I am forty-one, and my pathologies sometimes feel so overwhelming that I am lucky just to get home at the end of the day. Luckier still if there is a hug waiting for me on the other side of the front door.

It was not always this way. When I was twenty-five, I thought I had faith dialed in. Most people thought I was a pretty great Christian. And unfortunately, I believed them.

I have a memory from my twenty-fifth year when I was walking west, down Monroe Avenue in Corvallis, Oregon, passing a fraternity, a coffee shop, and a convenience store. As I recall, I was not thinking about much at all. The sun was on my face, and my mind was drifting. And then it popped into my head. It was a single thought as clear as a rifle shot. The thought was this: *I am not sure I am even a sinner.* It is quite possibly the most shameful thought of my life.

Back in those days, I sometimes thought I had the religious game wired. I believed Jesus was pretty lucky to have me on his team. Back then, I thought we lived in a two-team world. I needed to believe this was so because I wanted to be a star on the God-team.

I don't believe in that world anymore.

I do believe in the gospel of Jesus Christ. It is the manifesto of my life.

The gospel is as simple as Jesus' phrase, "Follow me"—an idea that my four-year-old grasps (most days better than I do). The gospel is also so vast and so intricate that if every one of its stories were written down, I suppose that even the whole world would not have room for the books that would be written. It is the story of a broken world. It is the story of the pursuant God. It is the story of a beloved creation. It is the story of a sacrificial Savior. It is the story of making all things right.

Ultimately, everyone is looking for this story. They want to understand its themes and they want to know its implications: for their painful yesterdays, their struggling todays, and their hope-starved tomorrows.

It is God's story. He is a great communicator. He is the protagonist. He is the hero. He is the source. The problem is that most
days I am not sure if God and I are on speaking terms. Luckily, like
a good parent, God is patient with me. He is patient with us all.

God wants to share his story. And it is his pleasure where, how,
and to whom he reveals his story. In my life, more often than I have
wanted to admit, the themes of God's story have come from people
who did not wear my same religious uniform, did not have my same
spiritual name badge (Hello! My religion is . . .), and certainly did
not come from my same background or experiences. But they were
God's voice all the same.

In Albania I first learned to try and not limit God's creative
voice. In my "alone and away" years, I learned to submit to God's
healing from unexpected sources. At Reed College I got to rest in
my Jesus-faith, in and among a diverse faith community. And in my
neighborhood today, I am learning that ultimately my spiritual formation is found in our full-body incarnation in our very specific
time and place.

The *other* person is not my enemy. They are the hands of my
healing and the mouthpiece of my enlightenment.

When Jesus' closest friends wrote his story, they included his
lineage. It is found on the first pages of two of Jesus' life stories,
by Matthew and Luke. His lineage includes names like Joseph, his
adoptive father; King David; and Abraham. It also includes Rahab,
a foreign prostitute; and Ruth, a Moabite; alongside numerous
questionable characters, including murderers, adulterers, deceivers,
and doubters. They all get equal billing in the "opening credits" of
Jesus' life story.

When the story of my spiritual lineage is declared, it will certainly include my grandmother Gigi, my dad and my mom, as well
as numerous Christian mentors and friends. It will also boldly
and unapologetically include wise men like Fidnet, my Albanian

grandmother; my friend Luli; and an anonymous Muslim cleric. It will include Pope, Katarina, and Dennis the bartender; it will include Jared, Carlos, and a couple dozen Reed students who dreamed together on Thursday evenings; it will include Robbie and Bobbin . . . it will be filled with my neighbors.

May we stand together before the glorious sunset that is the gospel of Jesus Christ and explore it, admire it, and love it. May we learn together to say, "Woe am I" before the wonder of God. And in response to God's eternally creative voice, may we increasingly learn to submit our collective lives to him.

Let the epiphanies come. Amen.

SCRIPTURE REFERENCES

Introduction
Acts 17:27–28
Eph. 4:6
Col. 1:17

Chapter 2
2 Corin. 6:14
John 1:47,
    paraphrased

Chapter 3
John 20:27

Chapter 8
Luke 12:24, 27
Matt. 8:5–13
Gen. 1:26, emphasis
    added
Matt. 25:40, 35–36
Matt. 13:35 MSG

Chapter 14
Gen. 2:9
Gen. 1:29

Chapter 15
Matt. 23: 27

Chapter 16
John 1:14 MSG

Chapter 18
Matt. 25:40,
    paraphrased
Matt. 6:2, NASB
Gal. 3:28–29,
    paraphrased
Isa. 11:6–9,
    paraphrased
Jer. 31:34,
    paraphrased

Amos 5:24,
    paraphrased
Isa. 65:19–22,
    paraphrased

Chapter 19
Ps. 65:8 NASB

Chapter 23
Gen. 1:26
Gen 1:29–30
Luke 17:2

Chapter 24
Matt. 5:23–24
Mark 9:50, emphasis
    added
Rom. 12:18,
    paraphrased

ACKNOWLEDGMENTS

IT FEELS VERY OVERWHELMING TO ATTEMPT TO EXPRESS MY gratitude.

First, during the writing of this book, both my father and my grandma Gigi passed away. I am indebted to both of them for their profound contribution to my life and spirit. Alongside them are my mom and my sister as my lifelong supports and defenders. Thank you.

I am *most* grateful for my wife, Aimee, and our three young boys, for the love, encouragement, and meaning they infuse into my every day.

Also, thanks to our community of faith that walks with us through a life that extends far beyond a book project: our communal household, the Abbey, the Sabbath dinner gathering, and the men of Friday morning.

As for the process of writing, I find myself particularly thankful for Dan Elliott, who first planted the seed in me to write, and to Donald Miller, who spoke loving confidence into me that I could be published. Thanks to David Sanford and Matt Baugher, who got this particular project off the ground. And thank you to about three dozen beautiful folks who gave creative and editorial advice through the writing of this manuscript.

Finally, when you have lived a life like mine, there are few gifts as great as folks who support and believe in you consistently through good times and bad. There have been a few such people in my story. One couple that I would like to thank here are Don and Kathryn Mansfield. Across the twenty-one years that this book spans, they have defended me and have shared the weight of my failures, and for that I am forever grateful.

ABOUT THE AUTHOR

TONY KRIZ HAS AN EARNED DOCTORATE IN SPIRITUAL FORMATION. He is a teacher of faith and culture through the mass media, via social media, and at universities, conferences, and communities of faith.

Tony has served with a variety of international organizations, living much of that time in Eastern Europe ministering with Muslims in Albania and loving a war-torn former Yugoslavia.

Many were first introduced to Tony under the moniker "Tony the Beat Poet." He lived for a season alongside the radically liberal campus of Reed College in Portland; some of his exploits were first described in Donald Miller's best-selling book *Blue Like Jazz*.

Today, Tony journeys with a community of life-servants among some of Portland's most culturally diverse neighborhoods and lives in submission to a multiracial gathering of Jesus-followers. He is giving his time to transforming urban missions: nurturing the Parish Collective network, integrating a holistic gospel-life, and serving as coach/consultant for church planters from diverse traditions.

Tony lives with his wife, Aimee, and their three sons (Malachi, Hudson, and Tristan) in an intentional community of faith. Together they have been foundational participants of several spiritual communities that serve the disillusioned, artistic, and dramatically post-Christian cultures of east Portland.

For more information, visit www.tonykriz.com.